Utilize este código QR para se cadastrar de forma mais rápida:

Ou, se preferir, entre em:
www.richmond.com.br/ac/livroportal
e siga as instruções para ter acesso aos conteúdos exclusivos do
Portal e Livro Digital

CÓDIGO DE ACESSO:
A 00096 TBIENGK1E 4 11953

Faça apenas um cadastro. Ele será válido para:

From trees to books,
sustainability all the way

Da semente ao livro,
sustentabilidade por todo o caminho

Planting forests

The wood used as raw material for our paper comes from planted forests, that is, it is not the result of deforestation. This practice generates thousands of jobs for farmers and helps to recover environmentally degraded areas.

Plantar florestas

A madeira que serve de matéria-prima para nosso papel vem de plantio renovável, ou seja, não é fruto de desmatamento. Essa prática gera milhares de empregos para agricultores e ajuda a recuperar áreas ambientais degradadas.

Making paper and printing books

The entire paper production chain, from pulp production to book binding, is certified, complying with international standards for sustainable processing and environmental best practices.

Fabricar papel e imprimir livros

Toda a cadeia produtiva do papel, desde a produção de celulose até a encadernação do livro, é certificada, cumprindo padrões internacionais de processamento sustentável e boas práticas ambientais.

Creating content

Our educational solutions are developed with life-long goals guided by editorial values, diverse viewpoints and socio-environmental responsibility.

Criar conteúdos

Os profissionais envolvidos na elaboração de nossas soluções educacionais buscam uma educação para a vida pautada por curadoria editorial, diversidade de olhares e responsabilidade socioambiental.

Developing life projects

Richmond educational solutions are an act of commitment to the future of younger generations, enabling partnerships between schools and families in their mission to educate!

Construir projetos de vida

Oferecer uma solução educacional Richmond é um ato de comprometimento com o futuro das novas gerações, possibilitando uma relação de parceria entre escolas e famílias na missão de educar!

Scan the QR code to learn more.
Access *https://mod.lk/rich_sus*

Fotografe o código QR e conheça melhor esse caminho.
Saiba mais em *https://mod.lk/rich_sus*

THE BIG IDEA

English for Kids

4

Editora responsável:
Izaura Valverde

Richmond

Direção editorial: Sandra Possas

Edição executiva de inglês: Izaura Valverde
Edição executiva de produção e multimídia: Adriana Pedro de Almeida

Coordenação de arte e produção: Raquel Buim
Coordenação de revisão: Rafael Spigel

Edição de texto: Carina Guiname Shiroma, Giuliana Gramani, Leila Scatena
Elaboração de conteúdo: Ana Cláudia Rodovalho, Carina Guiname Shiroma, Sílvia Beraldo
Preparação de originais: Helaine Albuquerque
Revisão: Carolina Waideman, Flora Vaz Manzione, Gisele Ribeiro Fujii, Kandy Saraiva, Katia Gouveia Vitale, Larissa Martin, Lucila Vrublevicius Segóvia, Márcia Suzumura, Márcio Martins, Marina Gomes, Ray Shoulder, Vivian Cristina de Souza

Projeto gráfico: Karina de Sá
Edição de arte: Priscila Wu
Diagramação: Casa de Ideias
Capa: Fabiane Eugenio
Ilustração da capa: Nicolas Maia
Ilustrações: Alexandre Matos, Artur Fujita, Carlitos Pinheiro, Carol Sartori, David Martins, Fábio Eugênio, Lais Bicudo, Laurent Cardon, Leo Teixeira, Marcus Penna, Michel Ramalho, Oldrine, Oli, Thiago Neumann
Artes: Priscila Wu

Real-Time View (RTV): Gabrielle Navarro (edição de conteúdo); Amanda Miyuki, Mônica M. Oldrine (*design*); Gislaine Caprioli, Letícia Della Giacoma de França (revisão)
Portal Educacional Richmond: Gabrielle Navarro (edição e curadoria de conteúdo); Maria Eduarda Scetta (curadoria de conteúdo); Amanda Miyuki (*design*); Eloah Cristina (analista de projeto); Gislaine Caprioli, Letícia Della Giacoma de França (revisão)
Adventureland: Gabrielle Navarro (elaboração e edição de conteúdo); Daniel Favalli (produção); Mônica M. Oldrine (*design*); Gislaine Caprioli, Letícia Della Giacoma de França (revisão)
Digital Academy for Kids: Gabrielle Navarro (elaboração e edição de conteúdo); Daniel Favalli (produção); Mônica M. Oldrine (*design*); Gislaine Caprioli, Letícia Della Giacoma de França (revisão)
Livro Digital Interativo: Gabrielle Navarro (edição de conteúdo); Daniel Favalli (produção); Mônica M. Oldrine (*design*); Gislaine Caprioli, Letícia Della Giacoma de França (revisão)
Livro Digital para Projeção: Gabrielle Navarro (edição de conteúdo); Amanda Miyuki (*design*); Eloah Cristina (analista de projeto); Gislaine Caprioli, Letícia Della Giacoma de França (revisão)

Iconografia: Danielle Alcântara, Ellen Silvestre, Eveline Duarte, Paloma Klein, Sara Alencar
Coordenação de *bureau*: Rubens M. Rodrigues
Tratamento de imagens: Ademir Francisco Baptista, Joel Aparecido, Luiz Carlos Costa, Marina M. Buzzinaro, Vânia Aparecida M. de Oliveira
Pré-impressão: Alexandre Petreca, Everton L. de Oliveira, Fabio Roldan, Marcio H. Kamoto, Ricardo Rodrigues, Vitória Sousa
Áudio: Núcleo de Criação Produções em Áudio

Todos os *sites* mencionados nesta obra foram reproduzidos apenas para fins didáticos. A Richmond não tem controle sobre seu conteúdo, o qual foi cuidadosamente verificado antes de sua utilização.

Websites mentioned in this material were quoted for didactic purposes only. Richmond has no control over their content and urges care when using them.

Embora todas as medidas tenham sido tomadas para identificar e contatar os detentores de direitos autorais sobre os materiais reproduzidos nesta obra, isso nem sempre foi possível. A editora estará pronta a retificar quaisquer erros dessa natureza assim que notificada.

Every effort has been made to trace the copyright holders, but if any omission can be rectified, the publishers will be pleased to make the necessary arrangements.

Impressão e acabamento: HRosa Gráfica e Editora
Lote: 797801 **Cod:** 120002163

Dados Internacionais de Catalogação na Publicação (CIP)
(Câmara Brasileira do Livro, SP, Brasil)

The big idea : English for kids / obra coletiva concebida, organizada, desenvolvida e produzida pela Editora Moderna ; editora responsável Izaura Valverde. -- 1. ed. -- São Paulo : Moderna, 2021.

Obra em 5 v. para alunos do 1º ao 5º ano.

1. Inglês (Ensino fundamental) I. Valverde, Izaura.

21-65926 CDD-372.652

Índices para catálogo sistemático:
1. Inglês : Ensino fundamental 372.652
Cibele Maria Dias - Bibliotecária - CRB-8/9427

ISBN 978-65-5779-842-3 (LA)
ISBN 978-65-5779-843-0 (LP)

Reprodução proibida. Art. 184 do Código Penal e Lei 9.610 de 19 de fevereiro de 1998.
Todos os direitos reservados.

Richmond
Santillana Educação Ltda.
Rua Padre Adelino, 758, 3º andar – Belenzinho
São Paulo – SP – Brasil – CEP 03303-904
www.richmond.com.br
2024

Impresso no Brasil

Créditos das fotos: p. 8: Sunny studio/Shutterstock; p. 10: ADragan/iStockphoto, Africa Studio/Shutterstock, DONOT6/iStockphoto, manoonpan phantong/iStockphoto, gerenme/iStockphoto, Rawf8/iStockphoto, ra3rn/iStockphoto, frank600/iStockphoto; p. 12: YakobhukOlena/iStockphoto; p. 13: H. ARMSTRONG ROBERTS/Alamy/Fotoarena, Eisenlohr/iStockphoto, The Toidi/Shutterstock, philipimage/iStockphoto, CasPhotography/iStockphoto, Jesse Holanda/iStockphoto, scanrail/iStockphoto, focal point/Shutterstock, Vanit Janthra/iStockphoto, jakkapan21/iStockphoto, man_kukuku/iStockphoto, artapartment/Shutterstock, Business stock/Shutterstock, Biletskiy_Evgeniy/iStockphoto; p. 14: Dotta2; p. 16: Dimitri Otis/Getty Images, alle12/iStockphoto, deepblue4you/iStockphoto, scanrail/iStockphoto; p. 18: igorr1/iStockphoto, loops7/iStockphoto, bennymarty/Getty Images, AVTG/iStockphoto; p. 19: ajr_images/iStockphoto, NADOFOTOS/iStockphoto; p. 20: Prostock-Studio/Shutterstock, Syda Productions/Shutterstock, kottofei/iStockphoto, bortonia/iStockphoto; p. 21: nyschooter/iStockphoto, Kesu01/iStockphoto; p. 24: tamara Kaliuzhna/iStockphoto, malerapaso/iStockphoto, Africa Studio/Shutterstock; p. 25: RENGraphic/iStockphoto; p. 26: Willyam Bradberry/Shutterstock, Danita Delimont/Shutterstock, legna69/iStockphoto, afhunta/iStockphoto, Thorsten Spoerlein/iStockphoto, THEPALMER/iStockphoto, leungchopan/iStockphoto, karelnoppe/iStockphoto; p. 28: Paul_Cooper/iStockphoto, Matt Dirksen/iStockphoto, rabbit75_ist/iStockphoto, o2beat/iStockphoto, tzuky333/iStockphoto, AB Photography/iStockphoto, Pahis/iStockphoto, Tomwang112/iStockphoto, Lisa5201/iStockphoto, fizkes/iStockphoto, BraunS/iStockphoto, Imgorthand/iStockphoto; p. 29: Zuberka/iStockphoto, LeManna/iStockphoto, GeorgeVieiraSilva/Shutterstock, FatCamera/iStockphoto, SerrNovik/iStockphoto, Solovyova/iStockphoto, izusek/iStockphoto; p. 30: LittleBee80/iStockphoto, ErikMandre/iStockphoto, Paul Collins/iStockphoto, mseuters/Shutterstock; p. 31: Damocean/iStockphoto; p. 32: GeorgePeters/iStockphoto, webmink/iStockphoto, ands456/iStockphoto, Barberelli/iStockphoto, DJB/iStockphoto, EmilyNorton/iStockphoto; p. 34: John Lawson/Getty Images, monkeybusinessimages/iStockphoto, Juanmonino/iStockphoto, Pixpine/iStockphoto; p. 36: New Africa/Shutterstock, margostock/Shutterstock, Sergey Gerashchenko/iStockphoto, AVNphotolab/iStockphoto, artisteer/iStockphoto, AlenaMozhjer/iStockphoto, Lifestyle Travel Photo/Shutterstock, GoncharukMaks/Shutterstock, Red Moccasin/Shutterstock, glamour/Shutterstock, Iuliia Alekseeva/iStockphoto, AnEduard/Shutterstock, Studio Peace/Shutterstock, VLADIMIR/Shutterstock, roy james Shakespeare/Getty Images, blackday/iStockphoto, Svetlana Hristova/iStockphoto; p. 37: Xiao Cai/iStockphoto, SanneBerg/iStockphoto, PIUA/Shutterstock, Hakase_/iStockphoto; p. 38: Chadiyanto/Shutterstock, Ocskay Mark/iStockphoto, Alisa Haneli/Shutterstock, gpointstudio/iStockphoto, Alija/iStockphoto, grinvalds/iStockphoto, aldomurillo/iStockphoto, SerrNovik/iStockphoto; p. 39: THP Creative/iStockphoto, elenabs/iStockphoto, Ihor Biliavskyi/iStockphoto; p. 40: Mukhina1/iStockphoto, photoschmidt2017/iStockphoto, New Africa/Shutterstock; p. 41: Ensup/iStockphoto, Rawpixel Ltd. /iStockphoto, maybeiii/iStockphoto, Leszek Czerwonka/Shutterstock, lechatnoir/iStockphoto, grinvalds/iStockphoto, SusanaValera/iStockphoto, lovro77/iStockphoto, Danish Khan/iStockphoto, Leila Melhado/iStockphoto, Alexey_ds/iStockphoto, _jure/iStockphoto, monkeybusinessimages/iStockphoto, Odua Images/Shutterstock; p. 42: cleristonribeiro/iStockphoto; p. 44: Evrymmnt/Shutterstock, sklyareek/Shutterstock, AJ_Watt/iStockphoto, undefined undefined/iStockphoto; p. 46: Prostock-Studio/Getty Images, evgenyatamanenko/iStockphoto, monkeybusinessimages/iStockphoto, damircudic/iStockphoto, romrodinka/iStockphoto, photosaint/iStockphoto, JackF/iStockphoto, monkeybusinessimages/iStockphoto, MichaelSvoboda/iStockphoto, fizkes/iStockphoto, fotostorm/iStockphoto; p. 47: praetorianphoto/iStockphoto, dexter_s/iStockphoto, NicolasMcComber/iStockphoto, Prostock-sTUDIO/iStockphoto, LSOphoto/iStockphoto, Imgorthand/iStockphoto, ijubaphoto/iStockphoto, PeopleImages/iStockphoto, sneks/iStockphoto; p. 48: Dotta2, JackF/iStockphoto; p. 51: LeManna/iStockphoto, LeManna/Shutterstock; p. 52: Tatomm/iStockphoto, Africa Studio/iStockphoto, alvarez/iStockphoto, paikong/Shutterstock, OlegDoroshin/Shutterstock, ersinkisacik/iStockphoto, nikkytok/iStockphoto, anatoliy_gleb/iStockphoto, chokja/iStockphoto, Capuski/iStockphoto, Sannie32/iStockphoto; p. 54: Lunatictm/Shutterstock, ThomasVogel/iStockphoto, Africa Studio/Shutterstock, Sallehudin Ahmad/Shutterstock, Kuki Ladron de Guevara/Shutterstock, MileA/iStockphoto, jittawit21/Shutterstock, KewTJ/Shutterstock, ericcrama/iStockphoto, dorastock/Shutterstock; p. 55: PeopleImages/iStockphoto, Quality Stock Arts/Shutterstock, ARTYOORANS/Shutterstock; p. 56: IrenaV/Shutterstock, Mehmet Hilmi Barcin/iStockphoto, LUNAMARINA/iStockphoto, SeventyFour/iStockphoto; p. 57: setory/iStockphoto; p. 59: monkeybusinessimages/iStockphoto, Wavebreakmedia/iStockphoto; p. 60: shironosov/iStockphoto, Okssi68/iStockphoto, mixetto/iStockphoto, YakobchukOlena/iStockphoto, kali9/iStockphoto, Prostock-Studio/iStockphoto, Daizuoxin/iStockphoto; p. 61: AlexSecret/iStockphoto; p. 62: vitalssss/iStockphoto, XtockImages/iStockphoto; p. 64: Lesyy/iStockphoto, Fierman Much/Shutterstock, karamba70/iStockphoto, kiboka/iStockphoto, Oleg1824/Shutterstock, ozdigital/iStockphoto, nata_vkusidey/iStockphoto, nitrub/iStockphoto, ddukang/iStockphoto, rez-art/iStockphoto, Arx0nt/iStockphoto, wmaster890/iStockphoto, Tom Stewart/Getty Images, Wagner Soares/iStockphoto, JatmikaVision/iStockphoto; p. 66: delihayat/iStockphoto, Wildzero/Shutterstock, Almaje/iStockphoto, itsarasak thithuekthak/iStockphoto, Sorbis/Shutterstock, seamartini/iStockphoto; p. 67: seamartini/Getty Images; p. 69: ALEAIMAGE/iStockphoto, bhofack2/iStockphoto; p. 70: Imgorthand/Getty Images, CasarsaGuru/Getty Images; p. 72: Skyimages/iStockphoto, samirabdala/iStockphoto, dennisvdw/iStockphoto, IakovKalinin/iStockphoto, Murat_MIZRAK/iStockphoto, akrassel/iStockphoto, cicloco/iStockphoto, Thomas Faull/iStockphoto, GUSK ehf./iStockphoto, swissmediavision/iStockphoto; p. 73: Alexander Piragis/Shutterstock, lucentius/iStockphoto, Tunatura/iStockphoto, -GP-/iStockphoto, Rock and Wasp/Shutterstock, Hugh Sitton/Getty Images, Vladimir Kazakov/Shutterstock, Guenter Guni/iStockphoto; p. 74: Aleksandra Golubtsova/iStockphoto, AleksandarNakic/Getty Images, FatCamera/iStockphoto, DCrane/Shutterstock, Jefferson Bernardes/Shutterstock; p. 75: krblokhin/iStockphoto, ChristaBrunt/iStockphoto, Michael Zeigler/iStockphoto, Imgorthand/iStockphoto, Soft_Light/iStockphoto, AlenaPaulus/iStockphoto; p. 76: kavram/iStockphoto, sumos/iStockphoto, FG Trade/iStockphoto, skiserge1/iStockphoto, Totajla/iStockphoto, iacomino FRiMAGES/Shutterstock; p. 77: SeamPavonePhoto/iStockphoto, Tsepova_Ekaterina/iStockphoto, Like Abrahams/iStockphoto, Dalphine Poggianti/iStockphoto, Brasil2/iStockphoto, anurakpong/iStockphoto, Eduardo Frederiksen/iStockphoto, richcarey/iStockphoto, Katarzyna Bialasiewicz/iStockphoto; p. 78: StockRocket/iStockphoto, Eugene Sergeev/iStockphoto; p. 79: Priyono/iStockphoto, wedekiba/iStockphoto, ailtonsza/iStockphoto, filipefrazao/iStockphoto, MSMcCarthy_Photography/iStockphoto, bogdanhoria/iStockphoto, Ababsolutum/iStockphoto, Lukasz Janyst/iStockphoto; p. 81: Inside Creative House/iStockphoto, SpiffyJ/iStockphoto; p. 82: aSuruwataRi/Shutterstock, Nobilior/iStockphoto, Marti57900/iStockphoto, ppart/iStockphoto, tobkatrina/iStockphoto, kedrov/Shutterstock, Tarzhanova/iStockphoto, Sashkinw/iStockphoto, ruzanna/iStockphoto, Africa Studio/Shutterstock, kyoshino/iStockphoto, netopaek/iStockphoto; p. 83: Kobby Dagan/Shutterstock, wrangel/iStockphoto; p. 85: CasarsaGuru/iStockphoto, pinstock/iStockphoto, polya_olya/Shutterstock, Goads Agency/iStockphoto, Ridofranz/iStockphoto, Hispanolistic/iStockphoto, kkshepel/iStockphoto, Jovanmandic/iStockphoto, Ridofranz/iStockphoto, SerrNovik/iStockphoto, Dotta 2, pooppiik/iStockphoto; p. 86: Nopadol Uengbunchoo/iStockphoto , Vima/iStockphoto, CGGissemann/iStockphoto, zoranm/iStockphoto, yasushiroamano/iStockphoto, novadream/iStockphoto, Paul_Brighton/iStockphoto, sbossert/iStockphoto, AdShooter/iStockphoto, gbh007/iStockphoto, rez-art/iStockphoto; p. 94: DZM/iStockphoto; p. 99: Wileydoc/Shutterstock, Askolds/iStockphoto, Sergey Pavlov/iStockphoto, kirza/iStockphoto, Hung Chung Chih/Shutterstock, MaksimYremenko/iStockphoto; p. 105: imaginima/iStockphoto, delihayat/iStockphoto, chapay/iStockphoto, RTimages/iStockphoto, Donna Beeler/Shutterstock, Serdar Tibet/Shutterstock, Portugal2004/iStockphoto, scanrail/iStockphoto; p. 107 Andrii Shelenkov/iStockphoto; p. 108: Towawww/iStockphoto, Mumemories/iStockphoto, rusm/iStockphoto, nipastock; p. 109: DamianKuzdak/iStockphoto, inkret/iStockphoto, Masha Rasputina/iStockphoto, HakuNellies/iStockphoto, georgeclerk/iStockphoto, BrianLasenby/iStockphoto, Christopher Jones/iStockphoto, SDI Productions/iStockphoto, Imgorthand/iStockphoto, SerrNovik/iStockphoto; p. 111: Lazy_Bear/iStockphoto, FangXiaNue/iStockphoto, Ljupco Smokovski/Shutterstock, kali9/iStockphoto; p. 113: Dean Mitchell/iStockphoto, shapecharge/iStockphoto, Bigandt_Photography/iStockphoto, monkeybusinessimages/iStockphoto, PeopleImages/iStockphoto, monkeybusinessimages/iStockphoto, CasarsaGuru/iStockphoto, Tetiana Soares/iStockphoto, katleho Seisa/iStockphoto, Louis-Paul St-Onge/iStockphoto, SDI Productions/iStockphoto, tylim/iStockphoto, AndreyPopov/iStockphoto, JohnnyGreig/iStockphoto, Maria Savenko/Shutterstock, LightField Studios/Shutterstock, SDI Productions/iStockphoto, Wavebreakmedia/iStockphoto, Morsa Images/iStockphoto, CGN089/Shutterstock; p. 117: IgorDutina/iStockphoto, Buzz Factory/iStockphoto, mphillips007/iStockphoto, Wagner Soares/iStockphoto, ViktoriiaNovokhatska/iStockphoto, Joao Mello/iStockphoto, margouillatphotos/iStockphoto, rudisill/iStockphoto; p. 120: SOL STOCK/iStockphoto, SrdjanPavlovic/iStockphoto, Nicholas Lamontanaro/Shutterstock, Bicho_raro/iStockphoto, mihtiander/iStockphoto, Gestur Leo Gislason/iStockphoto; p. 129: onurdongel/iStockphoto, tolgart/iStockphoto, Cozine/Shutterstock, eternalcreative/iStockphoto, Africa Studio/Shutterstock, grinvalds/iStockphoto, Chainarong Prasertthai/iStockphoto, JazzIRT/iStockphoto; p. 131: Riska/iStockphoto, Quality Stock Arts/Shutterstock, ASIFE/iStockphoto, C.Lotungkum/Shutterstock, digitalskillet/iStockphoto, Hafizussalam bin Sulaiman/Shutterstock, yacobchuk/iStockphoto, Micha/Shutterstock, Audy_indy/iStockphoto, Hajohoos/iStockphoto, kenkuza/Shutterstock, artstore/Shutterstock; p. 133: Drozhzhina Elena/Shutterstock, Anthony Paz/iStockphoto, Dadid Kadlec/iStockphoto, GEORGIY DATSENKO/iStockphoto, Maren Winter/iStockphoto, GMWozd/iStockphoto, October22/iStockphoto, Moncherie/iStockphoto.

Contents

Scope and Sequence **4**

Welcome **6**

UNIT **1**
Contact Is Key **8**

Here and Now **15**

UNIT **2**
All Year Round **16**

CLIL **23**   Review 1 & 2 **24**

UNIT **3**
Incredible Animals **26**

Here and Now **33**

UNIT **4**
What I Wear **34**

CLIL **41**   Review 3 & 4 **42**

UNIT **5**
The Time Is Now **44**

Here and Now **51**

UNIT **6**
Daily Routine **52**

CLIL **59**   Review 5 & 6 **60**

UNIT **7**
It's on the Menu **62**

Here and Now **69**

UNIT **8**
In the Wild **70**

CLIL **77**   Review 7 & 8 **78**

Hands On **82**

Games **88**

Instructions **92**

Language Reference **93**

Glossary **102**

Workbook **105**

Press-outs **121**

Stickers **129**

Scope and Sequence

Unidade	Objetivos	Conteúdo linguístico	Conteúdo digital	Gênero textual	CLIL / Here and Now	Apêndices
Welcome – p. 6							
1 Contact Is Key p. 8	▶ Falar sobre diferentes meios de comunicação. ▶ Descrever onde determinados objetos estão localizados. ▶ Escrever uma mensagem de texto. ▶ Identificar um diagrama e decifrar seu conteúdo. ▶ Criar um diagrama.	computer, letter, magazine, newspaper, radio, smartphone, telephone, TV; behind, between, in, in front of, next to, on, under Where is (the TV)? / Where are (the letters)? It's (on the wall). / They're (behind the couch). There is (one letter). / There are (two radios).	Vídeo: An augmented world	diagrama	**Here and Now:** Mindfulness para evitar conflitos de comunicação.	**Workbook** p. 105
2 All Year Round p. 16	▶ Falar sobre meses e estações do ano. ▶ Descrever condições de tempo atmosférico. ▶ Contar até 69. ▶ Perguntar e responder sobre a idade de alguém. ▶ Identificar e localizar informações em um calendário. ▶ Elaborar um calendário.	January, February, March, April, May, June, July, August, September, October, November, December; cloudy, cold, hot, rainy, snowy, sunny, warm, windy; spring, summer, fall, winter; numbers 31-69 How old is he/she? He/She is (forty years old). What's the weather like? It's (cold and sunny). The temperature is (15) degrees Celsius.	Jogo: estações do ano e clima	calendário	**CLIL: Matemática** – Temperaturas em Celsius.	**Workbook** p. 107 **Hands On** p. 80
Review 1 & 2 – p. 24							
3 Incredible Animals p. 26	▶ Falar sobre animais e habilidades. ▶ Entrevistar colegas. ▶ Identificar e localizar informações em um texto informativo. ▶ Escrever um texto informativo.	bear, beaver, fox, frog, hare, moose, raccoon, salamander, squirrel, wolf; climb, dance, draw, play the (musical instrument), play (sport), ride a bike/horse, roller-skate, run, sing, swim Can you/they (play soccer)? Yes, I/they can. / No, I/they can't. I/He/She/They can (sing), but I/he/she/they can't (dance).	Quiz: animais e habilidades	texto informativo	**Here and Now:** Resiliência.	**Workbook** p. 109
4 What I Wear p. 34	▶ Perguntar e responder sobre vestuário. ▶ Descrever o que está vestindo e o que outras pessoas estão vestindo. ▶ Identificar e localizar informações em slogans. ▶ Escrever um slogan.	cap, dress, flip-flops, hat, jacket, jeans, shirt, shoes, shorts, skirt, sneakers, socks, sweater, T-shirt; old, new, big, small, long, short What are you wearing? I am wearing (a hat). What is he/she wearing? He/She is wearing (a jacket). Is he/she wearing (flip-flops)? Yes, he/she is. / No, he/she isn't. Are they wearing (shorts)? Yes, they are. / No, they aren't.	Infográfico: vestuário	slogan	**CLIL: Geografia** – Produção, circulação e consumo.	**Workbook** p. 111 **Hands On** p. 82
Review 3 & 4 – p. 42							

Unidade	Objetivos	Conteúdo linguístico	Conteúdo digital	Gênero textual	CLIL / Here and Now	Apêndices
5 **The Time Is Now** p. 44	▸ Descrever o que está ou não fazendo e o que outras pessoas estão ou não fazendo. ▸ Identificar e localizar informações em mensagens de texto. ▸ Escrever mensagens de texto.	clean, cook, do homework, drink, eat, listen to music, play video games, read, skateboard, sleep, study, take a shower, talk, use the computer, watch TV, work *What are you/they doing? I am/ am not (listening to music). / They are/aren't (watching TV).* *What is he/she doing? He/She is/ isn't (studying).* *Are you (cooking)? Yes, I am. / No, I'm not.*	Vídeo: *Safe internet*	mensagem de texto	**Here and Now:** *Mindfulness* para melhorar a concentração.	**Workbook** p. 113
6 **Daily Routine** p. 52	▸ Perguntar e dizer as horas. ▸ Falar sobre ações de rotina em progresso. ▸ Identificar e localizar informações em um bilhete. ▸ Escrever um bilhete.	a.m., p.m.; o'clock; midday, midnight; get up, go to bed, have breakfast/lunch/dinner *What time is it? It's (five o'clock). It's (seven o'clock) and I'm (having dinner).*	Vídeo: *Missing Monday morning*	bilhete	**CLIL: Matemática** – Medidas de tempo.	**Workbook** p. 115 **Hands On** p. 84

Review 5 & 6 – p. 60

Unidade	Objetivos	Conteúdo linguístico	Conteúdo digital	Gênero textual	CLIL / Here and Now	Apêndices
7 **It's on the Menu** p. 62	▸ Fazer pedidos em lanchonetes e restaurantes. ▸ Perguntar e responder sobre preços. ▸ Contar até 100. ▸ Identificar e localizar informações em um cardápio. ▸ Elaborar um cardápio.	apple pie, cheeseburger, chocolate cake, French fries, hamburger, hot dog, ice cream, onion rings, orange juice, salad, smoothie, soda; numbers 70-100 *How can I help you? I'd like a (soda)/an (orange juice)/ (French fries), please.* *How much is (the ice cream)/are (the onion rings)? It's/They're (five dollars).*	GIF: comida	cardápio	**Here and Now:** Abertura ao novo.	**Workbook** p. 117 **Hands On** p. 86
8 **In the Wild** p. 70	▸ Falar sobre atividades de aventura na natureza. ▸ Identificar e localizar informações em um folheto. ▸ Elaborar um folheto.	cave, glacier, jungle, ocean, river, swamp, volcano, waterfall; climb, cross, dive, explore, hike, sail, swim, visit *What is he/she doing? He/She is/isn't (exploring a cave).* *What are they doing? They are/ aren't (diving in the ocean).*	Jogo de tabuleiro: aventuras na natureza	folheto	**CLIL: Geografia** – Conservação e degradação da natureza.	**Workbook** p. 119

Review 7 & 8 – p. 78

Games – p. 88   **Instructions** – p. 92   **Language Reference** – p. 93   **Glossary** – p. 102   **Press-outs** – p. 121   **Stickers** – p. 129

five 5

Welcome

1 Press out and play.

seven

UNIT 1

Contact Is Key

1 Look and circle.

The child is…

1 sad.
2 tired.
3 surprised.
4 happy.

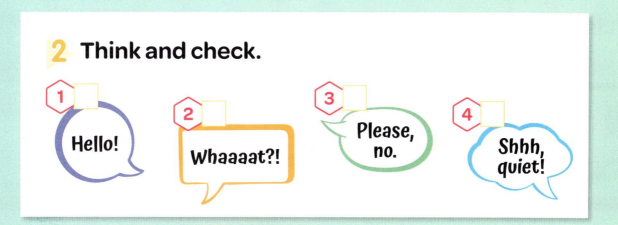

UNIT 1

3 Listen and say.

1. a computer

2. a letter

3. a magazine

4. a newspaper

5. a radio

6. a smartphone

7. a telephone

8. a TV

EXPLORE

The smartphone is **between** the magazine and the schoolbag.

The letter is **under** the magazine.

The smartphone is **on** the newspaper.

The computer is **next to** the schoolbag.

The schoolbag is **in front of** the TV.

The magazine is **behind** the letter. They are **in** the schoolbag.

10 ten

4 Listen and stick.

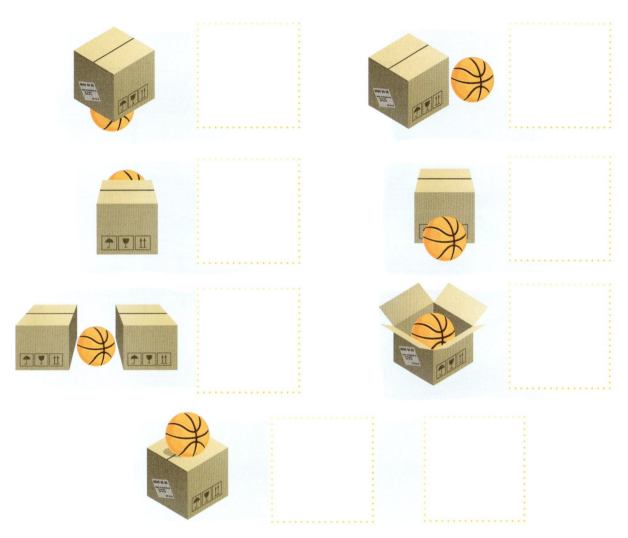

5 Listen and check.

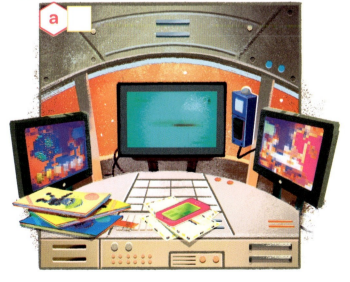

EXPLORE

6 Look and practice.

computer   letters   magazines   radio   smartphone

behind   between   in front of   next to   on   under

7 Read and circle.

1 The chair is in front **of** / **to** the desk.
2 Where **is** / **are** the magazine?
3 **There is** / **There are** three computers in the house.
4 Where **is** / **are** the TVs?
5 **There is** / **There are** a tablet on the desk.
6 The books are next **of** / **to** the radio.

8 **Look and check.**

1 This text is a…

  a ☐ diary. b ☐ diagram. c ☐ story.

2 The objective of the text is to…

  a ☐ tell a story. b ☐ show beautiful pictures. c ☐ give information.

3 In this kind of text, there are…

  a ☐ long sentences. b ☐ many words. c ☐ images.

9 **Read and circle.**

> The best title for this text is "The **advantages / evolution / problems** of communication".

10 Read again and check.

a ☐ The smartphone and the tablet represent the evolution of different equipment.

b ☐ The TV, the radio, the telephone and the camera are old equipment that we don't use today.

Learn more!
http://mod.lk/fai4_u1

11 Research and create.

12 Press out and stick. Then play a game.

14 fourteen

Mindfulness for Avoiding Communicative Conflicts

1. Look and talk.

2. Meditate.

3. Write and share.

UNIT 2
All Year Round

1 Look and match.

1. 🌧 2.  ☀ 3. ❄

a. (sunglasses) b. (boots) c. (umbrella)

2 Look, think and draw.

seventeen 17

3. Read, think and match.

a January, February — winter

b March, April, May — spring

c June, July, August — summer

d September, October, November — fall

December

4. Listen and say.

5. Listen, look and check your answers.

6 Listen and say.

 **10** ten  **20** twenty **30** thirty

40 forty **50** fifty **60** sixty

 7 Listen and circle.

1	3	13	**4**	16	60
2	14	40	**5**	44	46
3	15	50	**6**	52	58

8 Write the numbers in full.

1 — 49 — He's ___ years old.

2 — 32 — She's ___ years old.

nineteen 19

9 Listen and say. Then practice.

What's the weather like in the **summer**?

What's the weather like today?

It's **rainy** and **warm**.

It's **sunny** and **cold**.

sunny cloudy rainy snowy windy hot warm cold

10 Listen and check.

11 Look and circle.

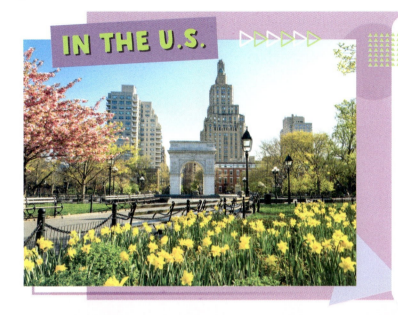

IN THE U.S.

MAY

S	M	T	W	T	F	S
		1	2	3	4	5
6	7	8	9	10	11	12
13	14	15	16	17	18	19
20	21	22	23	24	25	26
27	28	29	30	31		

Celebrations and Holidays:
13 – Mother's Day | 28 – Memorial Day

MAY

S	M	T	W	T	F	S
		1	2	3	4	5
6	7	8	9	10	11	12
13	14	15	16	17	18	19
20	21	22	23	24	25	26
27	28	29	30	31		

Celebrations and Holidays:
1 Labor Day | 13 – Mother's Day

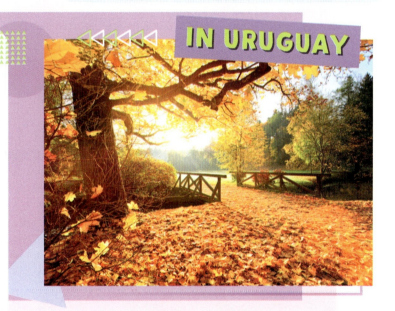

IN URUGUAY

The two texts are **letters / pages of a calendar / stories**.

12 Read and check.

In this kind of text, you can find…

a ☐ the days of the week.

b ☐ things you have to do.

c ☐ the name of the month.

d ☐ holidays.

e ☐ the time of your activities.

Learn more!
http://mod.lk/fai4_u2

twenty-one 21

13 Read again and complete.

1 There are _____ days in May.
2 The celebrations and holidays are colored in _____ in the calendars.
3 Labor Day is on May _____ in Uruguay.
4 Memorial Day is on May _____ in the U.S.
5 Mother's Day is on the same _____ in the U.S. and in Uruguay.
6 In May, it's _____ in Uruguay and spring in the U.S.

14 Make a calendar.

15 Draw and write.

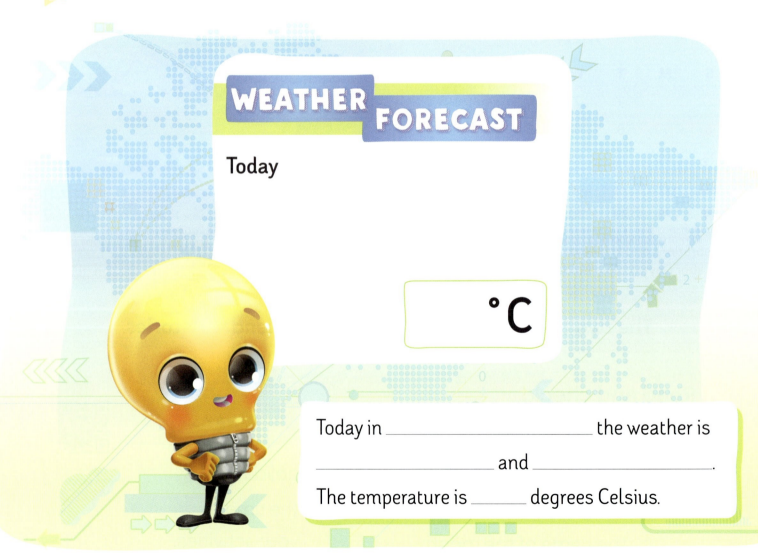

WEATHER FORECAST

Today

°C

Today in _____ the weather is _____ and _____.
The temperature is _____ degrees Celsius.

CLIL Temperatures in Celsius (Math)

1 Read and talk.

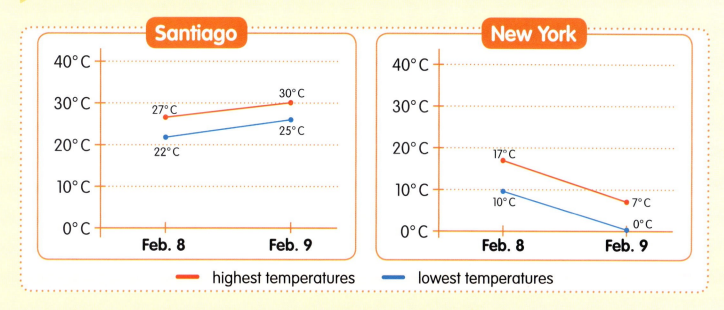

2 Read and complete.

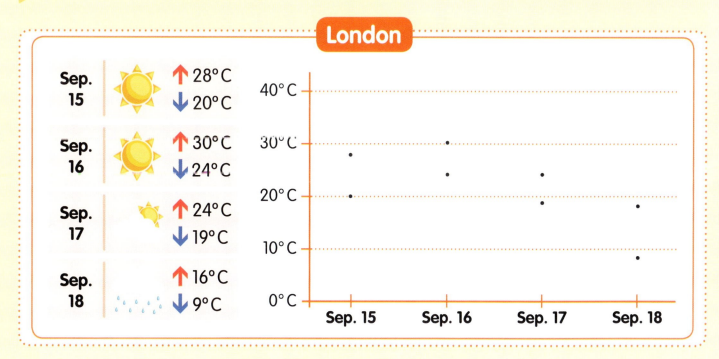

3 Research and make a graph.

Review 1 & 2

1 Complete the words.

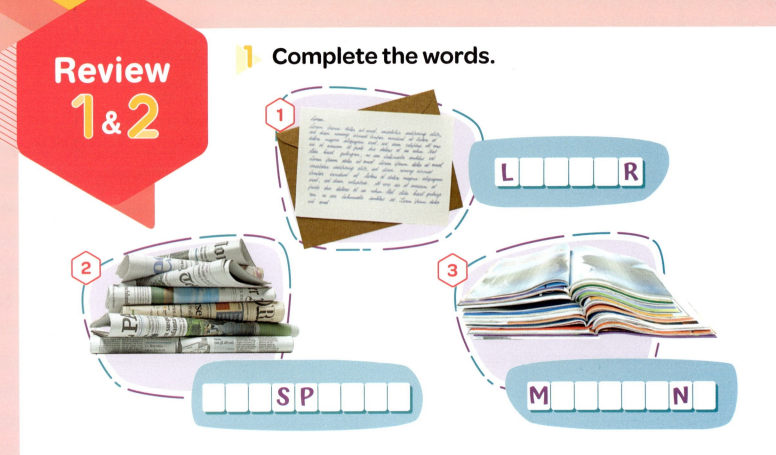

1. L _ _ _ _ R
2. _ _ S P _ _ _ _
3. M _ _ _ _ _ N

2 Look and complete.

Where is the tablet?

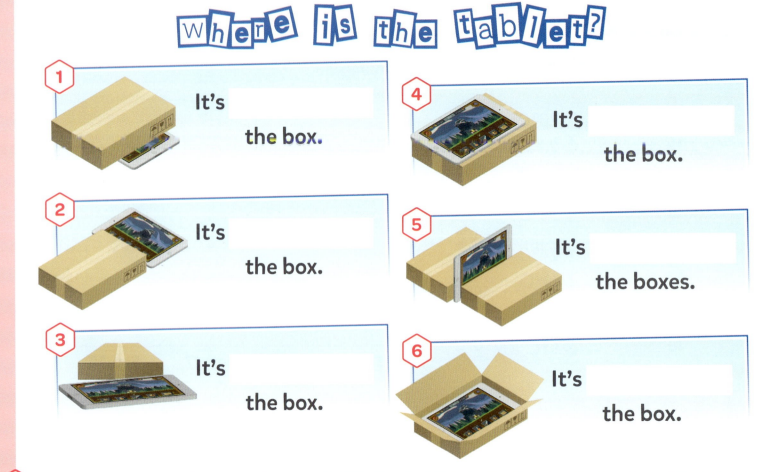

1. It's _____ the box.
2. It's _____ the box.
3. It's _____ the box.
4. It's _____ the box.
5. It's _____ the boxes.
6. It's _____ the box.

3 Look, read and match.

4 Read and answer.

1 How old are your parents?

_____

2 What's your favorite season?

_____

UNIT 3
Incredible Animals

1 **Look, think and guess.**

2 **Think and check.**

What are pandas' favorite food?

1 ☐ Fish.
2 ☐ Honey.
3 ☐ Bamboo.
4 ☐ Insects.
5 ☐ Banana.

twenty-seven 27

UNIT 3

3 Listen and say.

1 a frog

2 a moose

3 a raccoon

4 a salamander

5 a squirrel

6 a wolf

4 Think and check. Then listen.

climb trees

run fast

dance / sing

play

swim

1 Moose can…
  a ☐ climb trees.   b ☐ run fast.

2 Frogs can…
  a ☐ sing.   b ☐ run fast.

3 Raccoons can…
  a ☐ sing.   b ☐ swim.

4 Salamanders can…
  a ☐ dance.   b ☐ sing.

5 Squirrels can…
  a ☐ climb trees.   b ☐ sing.

6 Wolves can…
  a ☐ play.   b ☐ dance.

EXPLORE

He **can** dance.

She **can't** roller-skate.

Can you **climb** trees?

Yes, I can.

No, I can't.

 5 **Write and listen.**

draw   play handball   play soccer   play the drums
play the guitar   ride a bike   ride a horse   roller-skate

UNIT 3

6 Listen and say. Then talk.

Can you draw?

Yes, I can.

Can you play the drums?

No, I can't.

Can you...

	👍	👎
draw?	☐	☐
play soccer?	☐	☐
play the drums?	☐	☐
ride a bike?	☐	☐
ride a horse?	☐	☐
roller-skate?	☐	☐

EXPLORE

Bears can climb trees, **but** they can't sing.

Hares can run fast, **but** they can't dance.

Foxes can swim, **but** they can't draw.

7 Write and circle.

1 My classmate can _____,

but **he** / **she** can't _____.

2 I can _____,

but I can't _____.

30 thirty

8 Look and circle.

Sloths

Sloths live in the tropical forests of Central and South America. They are mammals and they sleep up to 20 hours a day!

Sloths have small ears and long arms. They can swim very well. Some sloths have two extra neck bones, so they can move their heads all the way around.

Sloths are small animals. They are about 60 to 80 centimeters. They are herbivores. Sloths live in the trees and they almost never get down. They can live for about 20 years and they can weigh 3 to 7 kilos.

Based on <https://kids.nationalgeographic.com/animals/mammals/sloth/>; <https://www.worldwildlife.org/stories/why-are-sloths-slow-and-six-other-sloth-facts>. Accessed on February 19, 2021.

1 The text is...
  a a story.
  b a news article.
  c an informative text.

2 This text is...
  a in a book.
  b on a website.
  c in a newspaper.

9 Read and check.

The objective of the text is...

1. ☐ to show images of sloths.
2. ☐ to give information about sloths.
3. ☐ to tell a story of a sloth.

thirty-one 31

10 Read again and complete.

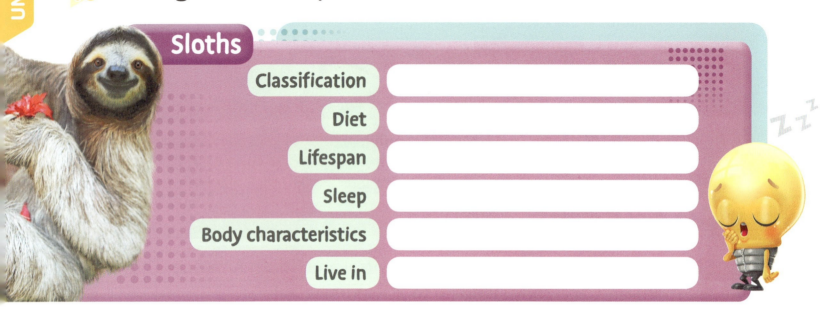

Sloths	
Classification	
Diet	
Lifespan	
Sleep	
Body characteristics	
Live in	

11 Research and write.

Learn more!
http://mod.lk/fai4_u3

12 Read and write *S* or *F*.

1. Beavers can build canals and water barrages.
2. Wood frogs can tolerate extremely cold temperatures.
3. Canadian salamanders can't sleep for more than 4 hours.
4. Foxes can't see in the dark.
5. Raccoons can't see colors very well.

HERE AND NOW

Resilience

1 **Look, read and talk.**

Beavers can swim.
Beavers can see underwater.
Beavers can hold their breath for 15 minutes underwater.
Beavers can cut down trees.

2 **Think and talk.**

3 **Think and share.**

UNIT 4
What I Wear

1 Look and point.

2 **Be creative and customize.**

UNIT 4

3 Listen and say.

 1 a cap
 2 a dress
 3 flip-flops
 4 a hat
 5 a jacket
 6 jeans
 7 a shirt
 8 shoes
 9 shorts
 10 a skirt
 11 sneakers
 12 socks
 13 a sweater
 14 a T-shirt

EXPLORE

What **are** you **wearing**?

I **am wearing** a purple T-shirt.

Is Lily **wearing** a dress?

Yes, she is.

Are they **wearing** flip-flops?

No, they aren't.

36 thirty-six

4 Complete and listen.

1. **A:** _____ Robin and Daniel _____ T-shirts?
   B: Yes, they _____. _____ _____ wearing T-shirts and blue shorts.

2. **A:** _____ is Charles _____?
   B: He _____ _____ brown shoes.

3. **A:** _____ René _____ a white cap?
   B: Yes, _____ _____.

4. **A:** _____ Mark _____ a jacket?
   B: No, _____ _____. He _____ _____ a sweater.

Learn more!
http://mod.lk/fai4_u4

5 Read, look and write.

6 Look and circle.

1. a) **old / new** brown shoes

   b) **old / new** black shoes

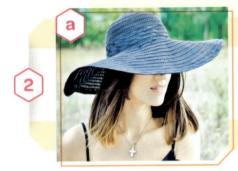
2. a) a **big / small** blue hat

   b) a **big / small** green hat

3. a) a **long / short** red dress

   b) a **long / short** yellow dress

7 Listen and say. Then practice.

She's wearing a new pink T-shirt.

It's this girl!

Correct! My turn!

He's wearing old blue jeans.

8 **Look and check.**

1 The texts are…
   a ☐ calendars.
   b ☐ slogans.
   c ☐ letters.

2 The objective of this kind of text is to…
   a ☐ make a list.
   b ☐ tell a story.
   c ☐ convince the reader to do something.

3 These texts are…
   a ☐ long.
   b ☐ short.
   c ☐ only images.

9 **Read and circle.**

The texts are about the **distribution / donation / production** of clothes and accessories.

thirty-nine 39

10 Read again and match.

1 Pass It On 2 Time To Donate 3 Warm Winter

a b c

11 Think and write.

12 Press out and play.

CLIL

Production, circulation and consumption (Geography)

1 Look and match.

2 Look and order.

3 Research and make a poster.

Review 3 & 4

1 Listen and circle.

Sofia: Grandpa, can you (1) **swim / draw**?

Grandpa: Yes, darling, I can. What about you? Can you (2) **swim / climb trees**?

Sofia: No, I (3) **can / can't**. But I can ride a (4) **horse / bike**!

Grandpa: Good! I (5) **can / can't** ride a bike. But I can (6) **ride a horse / play handball**.

Sofia: I can (7) **play handball / ride a horse** too. And can you (8) **draw / roller-skate**?

Grandpa: No! Ah, but I can play (9) **the guitar / basketball**!

Sofia: I can't play (10) **the guitar / basketball** or (11) **handball / the drums**.

Grandpa: But you can (12) **sing / draw** very well. You're an artist!

2 Read and complete.

Sofia can (1) _____ , (2) _____ and (3) _____ .

She can't (4) _____ , (5) _____ or (6) _____ .

3 Find and circle.

capdressflip-flopshatjacketjeansshirtshoesshorts

4 Match and complete.

big   long   new   old   small

1. Mark
2. Jake
3. Janice
4. Violet
5. Sheila

☐ This person is wearing socks, a cap and sneakers.

☐ This person is wearing a _____ sweater.

☐ This person is wearing _____ jeans and flip-flops.

☐ This person is wearing shorts and a _____ T-shirt.

☐ This person is wearing a _____ dress.

forty-three   43

UNIT 5
The Time Is Now

1 **Look, think and circle.**
   1 food   **2** fun   **3** music   **4** school   **5** sports

2 **Think and talk.**

indoors

outdoors

forty-five 45

3 Listen and say.

- a clean
- b cook
- c eat
- d listen to music
- e sleep
- f study
- g talk
- h use the computer

4 Listen and number.

EXPLORE

- What **are** you **doing**?
- I'm skateboarding.
- Lilly **isn't studying** at school.
- She's studying at home.
- Joe and Jill **aren't reading**.
- They're watching TV.

5 Look and complete.

listen   sleep   study   use

Anna _____ English.

Mark and Claire _____ to music.

The tiger _____.

Kiara and Ned _____ the computer.

6 Look, read and match.

a ☐ Julie is taking a shower.

b ☐ Dan and Dora are working.

c ☐ Jan and Bill are playing video games.

d ☐ Samuel is drinking orange juice.

e ☐ Will is doing homework.

forty-seven 47

7 Listen and say. Then practice.

8 Look and listen. Then mime and guess.

9 Look and circle.

1 The text is a series of...
   a text messages.
   b tests.
   c posts.

2 In this kind of text there are...
   a long paragraphs.
   b emojis and abbreviations.
   c illustrations.

3 The language of this kind of text is...
   a formal.
   b informal.

10 Read and check.

What is the text about?

1 ☐ The videos Alice is watching.
2 ☐ An important English test at school.
3 ☐ A friend asking for help with homework.

Learn more!
http://mod.lk/fai4_u5

11 Read again and complete.

1 _____ is watching videos.
2 _____ is doing the English homework.
3 _____ is asking for help.
4 _____ can help _____.
5 _____ is having problems with the activity on page 58.

12 Think and write.

13 Look and describe.

HERE AND NOW

Mindfulness to Improve Concentration

1. **Think and check.**

2. **Think and order.**

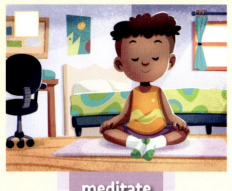
meditate

organize the room

play a relaxing song

sit properly

stretch

3. **Practice the actions.**

fifty-one 51

Daily Routine

UNIT 6

1. Look and check.

2. Think and circle.

fifty-two

fifty-three 53

3 Listen and say.

4 Listen, look and number.

9:00 = 9 o'clock
12:00 in the afternoon = midday
12:00 at night = midnight

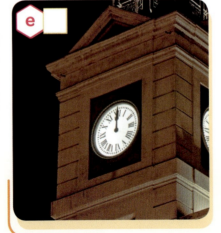

EXPLORE

It's eleven **a.m.**   What time is it?   It's eleven **p.m.**

5 **Read and stick.**

1. It's midnight.
2. It's ten p.m.
3. It's five o'clock.
4. It's three forty-five.
5. It's ten a.m.
6. It's seven fifteen.
7. It's midday.
8. It's eight thirty.

EXPLORE

I am **getting up**. — 6:45 A.M.
I am **having breakfast**. — 7:00 A.M.

I am **doing homework**. — 10:30 A.M.
I am **having lunch**. — 12:00 P.M.

I am **having dinner**. — 8:30 P.M.
I am **going to bed**. — 10:00 P.M.

6 Read and complete.

1 It's _6 o'clock_ and I am getting up.
2 It's _____ and I am doing homework.
3 It's _____ and I am _____.
4 It's _____ and I am _____.

Learn more!
http://mod.lk/fai4_u6

7 Listen and say. Then practice.

Rio de Janeiro

— What time is it?
— It's six thirty.
— What are you doing?
— I'm doing homework. And you?

8 Look and check.

1. This text is…
   a ☐ a love letter.
   b ☐ a note.
   c ☐ an e-mail.

2. It is…
   a ☐ formal.
   b ☐ informal.
   c ☐ long.

3. The objective of this kind of text is to…
   a ☐ tell a story.
   b ☐ answer questions.
   c ☐ inform and ask questions.

9 Read and underline.

1. The note is to **Jen's mom** / **Jen** / **Julie** from **Jen's mom** / **Jen** / **Julie**.
2. The objective of this note is to **ask Jen about a cheese pizza** / **tell Jen about a surprise party** / **inform about Jen's birthday**.

10 Read again and answer.

1 What is there in the refrigerator? _____
2 What time is the party? _____
3 Where is the party? _____
4 Can Jen's mom drive? _____
5 What is Jen's mom doing today? _____
6 What presents is Jen's mom suggesting for Julie? _____

11 Think and write.

12 Play bingo.

2:30	2:45	3:30	3:45	4:00	4:15
5:00	5:15	8:00	8:15	9:30	9:45
10:00	10:30	11:15	11:45	12:00 a.m.	12:00 p.m.

CLIL

Units of Time (Math)

1 **Look and match.**

a ☐ one day
b ☐ one minute
c ☐ one hour

2 **Calculate and answer.**

1 How many minutes are there in half an hour? _____
2 How many minutes are there in two hours? _____
3 How many hours are there in two days? _____

3 **Read, calculate and complete.**

1 Sally is at soccer practice for ☐ hours. She is on the train for ☐ minutes.

2 Joe is at school for ☐ hours. He is on the bus for ☐ hour and ☐ minutes.

4 **Write and talk.**

fifty-nine 59

Review 5 & 6

1 **Look and write.**

1 _____ and _____ are talking.
2 _____ is listening to music.
3 _____ is cleaning.
4 _____ is cooking.
5 _____ and _____ are sleeping.
6 _____ is eating.

2 **Think and complete.**

 English.

3 Listen and circle.

1	a 4:05 p.m.	b 4:15 p.m.	c 4:45 p.m.
2	a 12:00 a.m.	b 12:00 p.m.	c 12:30 p.m.
3	a 1:00 p.m.	b 2:00 p.m.	c 12:00 p.m.
4	a 8:15 a.m.	b 8:45 a.m.	c 8:55 a.m.
5	a 12:00 a.m.	b 12:00 p.m.	c 1:00 a.m.
6	a 6:30 p.m.	b 7:30 p.m.	c 3:30 p.m.

4 Listen and stick. Then complete.

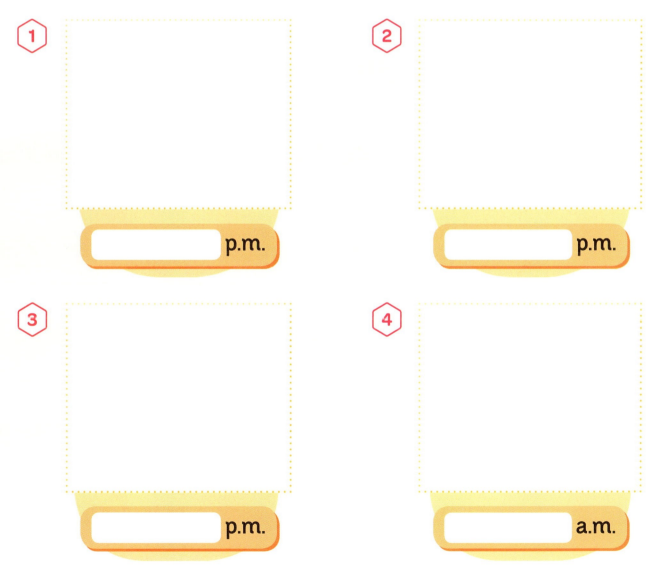

UNIT 7
It's on the Menu

1. Look and check.

1.
2.
3.

2. Choose and stick.

sixty-three 63

3 Listen and say.

a apple pie
b cheeseburger
c chocolate cake
d French fries
e hamburger
f hot dog
g ice cream
h onion rings
i orange juice
j salad
k smoothie
l soda

4 Listen and number.

EXPLORE

How can I help you?

I'd like **an** ice cream, please.

I'd like **a** salad, please.

How much is the hot dog?

It's $5.50.

How much are the smoothies?

They're $2.30.

5 Think and classify.

apple pie   cheeseburger   chocolate cake   hamburger
hot dog   orange juice   smoothie   soda

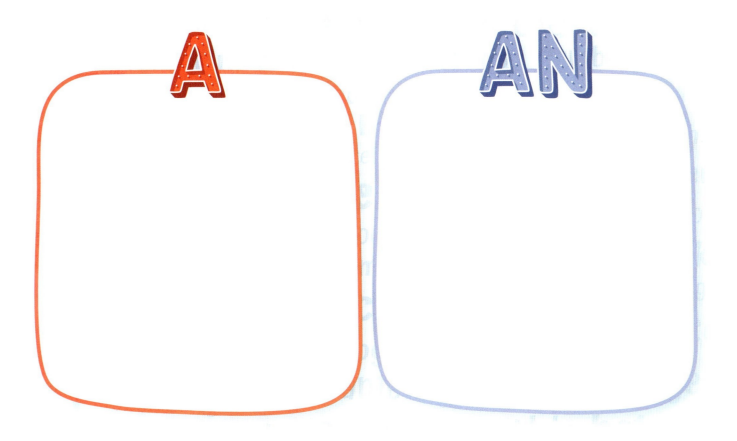

6 Think and complete.

1 **A:** How much _____ the onion rings?
   B: _____ $2.45.

2 **A:** How much _____ the apple pie?
   B: _____ $3.15.

3 **A:** How much _____ the chocolate cake?
   B: _____ $5.00.

4 **A:** How much _____ the French fries?
   B: _____ $4.20.

sixty-five 65

UNIT 7

7 Read and complete.

> 70 = seventy   80 = eighty   90 = ninety   100 = a hundred

1 $100.99 — The camera is _____ dollars and _____-nine cents.

2 $82.85 — The jacket is _____ dollars and _____ cents.

3 $1.75 — The ice cream is one dollar and _____ cents.

4 $91.79 — The guitar is _____ dollars and _____ cents.

8 Listen and say. Then practice.

FOOD
- HAMBURGER $5.70
- CHEESEBURGER $7.60
- FRENCH FRIES $4.45
- ONION RINGS $3.80

BEVERAGES
- ORANGE JUICE $2.95
- SODA $1.99

DESSERTS
- ICE CREAM $1.85
- CHOCOLATE CAKE $2.65

A: I'd like **a hamburger**, please.
B: Here you are.
A: How much **is it**?
B: **It's five** dollars and **seventy** cents.

66 sixty-six

9 **Look and circle.**

1 This is a **supermarket ad** / **recipe** / **menu**.

2 It includes **nutritional information about foods and drinks** / **a list of foods and drinks with prices** / **opinions on the foods and drinks**.

10 **Read and match.**

1	The name of the restaurant is…	a		Delicious Eats.
2	There is orange and…	b		of dessert.
3	There are three options…	c		lemon pie.
4	When you buy a combo, …	d		lemon juice.
5	There isn't…	e		a vegetarian option.
6	There is…	f		the soda is free.

11 Complete and calculate.

RECEIPT

Terminal #1   09-08-22

Item   Price

1x _____   _____

1x _____   _____

1x _____   _____

TOTAL AMOUNT   _____

THANK YOU

12 Create a menu.

13 Listen and role-play.

Server: How can I help you?

Customer: I'd like an orange juice, please.

Server: Here you are.

Customer: Thank you. How much is it?

Server: It's two dollars and seventy-three cents.

Customer: OK. Here it is. Thanks.

Server: Thank you very much! Have a nice day.

Open-mindedness

Learn more!
http://mod.lk/fai4_u7

▶1 **Think and check.**

▶2 **Look and talk.**

I like...
I don't like...
I want to try...

honey pancakes

toast with yeast extract

▶3 **Draw and share.**

sixty-nine 69

UNIT 8
In the Wild

1. **Look and circle.**

   1 in big cities **2** in nature **3** at home **4** at school

2. **Glue a photo.**

3 Listen and say.

1. a cave
2. a glacier
3. a jungle
4. an ocean
5. a river
6. a swamp
7. a volcano
8. a waterfall

4 Listen and circle.

1. explore caves 
2.  swim in waterfalls

5 Look and check.

seventy-two

6 **Look, read and match.**

1 c climb
2 ☐ cross
3 ☐ dive
4 ☐ explore
5 ☐ hike
6 ☐ sail
7 ☐ swim
8 ☐ visit

a   a cave
b   a river
c   ~~a volcano~~
d   a glacier
e   in the jungle
f   in the ocean
g   through a swamp
h   under a waterfall

7 **Look and write. Then listen.**

1 They are climbing a volcano.
2 _____
3 _____
4 _____
5 _____
6 _____
7 _____
8 _____

seventy-three 73

8 Look and circle.

She **is** / **isn't** climbing a mountain.   They **are** / **aren't** sailing in the river.

They **are** / **aren't** exploring the jungle.   He **is** / **isn't** crossing a swamp.

9 Listen and say. Then practice.

Learn more!
http://mod.lk/fai4_u8

What **is she** doing?

She is crossing a river.

What **are they** doing?

They are hiking in the jungle.

10 Look and underline.

1 This is a **diagram / leaflet / poster**.

2 The objective of this text is to **present plans / give information / tell a story**.

3 This kind of text usually **contains long texts / includes images / uses formal language**.

11 Read and order.

12 Read again and write *T* or *F*.

1. ☐ It costs $30 to visit the park.
2. ☐ Children can't go to the Yellow Mountain.
3. ☐ To visit the park, you need to access the website or call the park.
4. ☐ You can visit the park any day.
5. ☐ You can't camp in the park.

13 Research and create.

14 Think and check. Then talk.

On my vacation, I'd like to...

1. visit the Perito Moreno Glacier in Argentina.

2. climb a volcano in Iceland.

3. sail the Amazon river in Brazil.

4. swim under the Havasu waterfalls in the U.S.

5. explore the Jenolan Caves in Australia.

6. hike in the jungle in Costa Rica.

Conservation and Deterioration of Nature (Geography)

1. Look and talk.

Porto, Portugal

Cape Town, South Africa

Niagara Falls, Canada

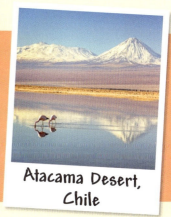
Atacama Desert, Chile

2. Think and check.

3. Research and create a poster.

Review 7 & 8

1 Listen and stick.

2 Read and order.

a ☐ **Server:** Here you are.
b ☐ **Server:** Thank you very much! Have a nice day!
c ☐ **Customer:** I'd like a hot dog, please.
d ☐ **Server:** It's one dollar and eighty-two cents.
e ☐ **Server:** How can I help you?
f ☐ **Customer:** Thank you. How much is it?
g ☐ **Customer:** OK. Here it is. Thanks.

3 **Look and write. Then complete.**

4 **Read and circle.**

1 John is climbing a **waterfall** / **volcano**.
2 Carol is **diving** / **exploring** in the ocean.
3 Chris is **climbing** / **sailing** a mountain.
4 Yasmin and Joshua are visiting a **glacier** / **river**.
5 My parents are **hiking** / **crossing** in the jungle.

Hands on

PRESENTING A WEATHER FORECAST

1. Talk about your favorite season.

2. Look and write.

dry   foggy   freezing   humid   stormy

3. Complete.

1. BR ⬜ ⬜ L
2. P ⬜ TUG ⬜
3. ⬜ GOL ⬜
4. TH ⬜ AND
5. ⬜ W ⬜ ALA ⬜ D
6. ⬜ ST ⬜ LIA
7. IN ⬜ A
8. C ⬜ AD ⬜
9. ⬜ PA ⬜
10. NO ⬜ AY

11. E ⬜ YP ⬜
12. ⬜ IJI
13. S ⬜ OA
14. ENG ⬜ ⬜ D
15. ⬜ ANCE
16. ⬜ GE ⬜ NA
17. C ⬜ NA
18. MO ⬜ C ⬜
19. ⬜ OUT ⬜ FR ⬜ ⬜
20. UN ⬜ D ⬜ TAT ⬜

4 Color.

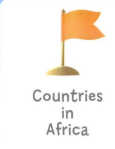

Countries in Africa | Countries in America | Countries in Asia | Countries in Australia and Oceania | Countries in Europe

5 Research.

Country: ______ Capital: ______

Continent: ______

What season is it now? ______

Month + day: ______

Weather forecast: ______

Temperature: ______

6 Make a poster.

7 Present a weather forecast.

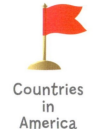

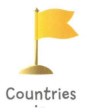

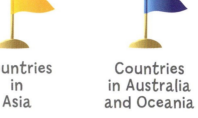

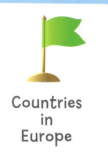

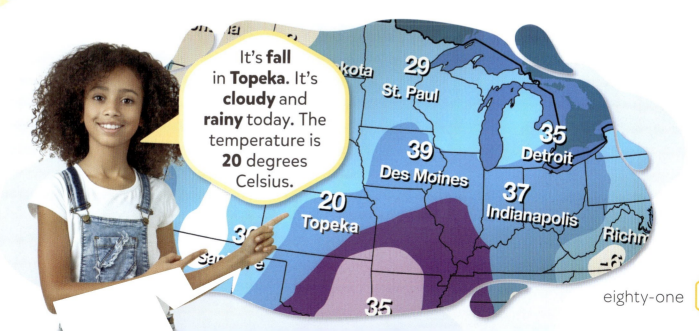

It's **fall** in **Topeka**. It's **cloudy** and **rainy** today. The temperature is **20** degrees Celsius.
29
St. Paul
39
Des Moines
35
Detroit
37
Indianapolis
20
Topeka
35

Hands on

1. Think and say.

2. Look and match.

| 1 makeup | 2 stockings | 3 mask | 4 cloak | 5 kimono |

| 6 scarf | 7 wig | 8 sandals | 9 crown |

| 10 fan | 11 vest | 12 boots |

3. Read, look and number.

1 **Shadow puppet theater**

It presents stories of great adventures or fantasy. The puppets are made from colored leather, with incredible detail.

2 *Kabuki* theater

It is famous for its red and white makeup and elaborate costumes. The colors of the makeup are important because they express the character's emotions.

4. Organize a play.

Play	Scenery	Characters

5. Perform a play.

Hands on

MAKING WORLD CLOCKS

1. Talk about your day.

2. Look and circle.

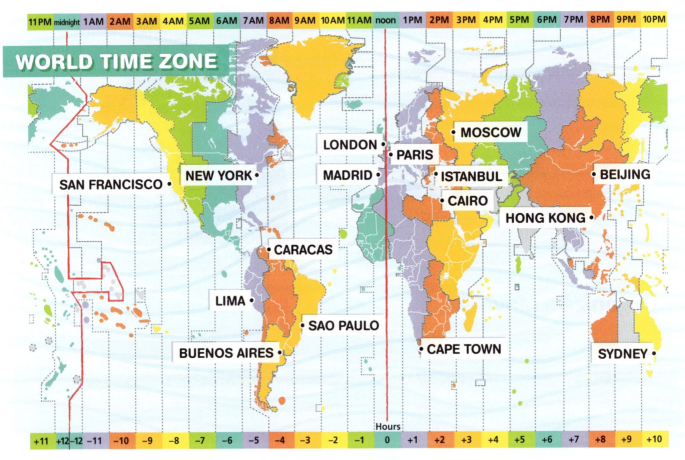

1. When it's 12:00 p.m. in London, it's **3:00 a.m. / 7:00 a.m.** in New York.
2. It's 12:00 p.m. in London and it's 8:00 p.m. in Beijing. So Beijing is **eight / three** hours ahead of London.
3. When it's 4:00 a.m. in San Francisco, it's **5:00 p.m. / 1:00 p.m.** in Paris.
4. When it's 9:00 a.m. in Sao Paulo, it's **10:00 p.m. / 1:00 p.m.** in Sydney.
5. It's 12:00 p.m. in London and it's 9:00 a.m. in Buenos Aires. So Buenos Aires is **five / three** hours behind London.

3 Look and complete.

1 Julia is **skateboarding** with friends in Istanbul. It's **2:00** p.m.
2 Paulo is _____ in Caracas. It's ____ a.m.
3 Maria is _____ in Lima. It's ____ a.m.
4 Bernardo is _____ in Moscow. It's ____ p.m.
5 Ross is _____ in Sydney. It's ____ p.m.
6 Juliet is _____ in Madrid. It's ____ p.m.
7 Sarah is _____ in Hong Kong. It's ____ p.m.
8 Matheus is _____ in Cape Town. It's ____ p.m.
9 Rania is _____ in Cairo. It's ____ p.m.
10 Joana is _____ with her friends in Sao Paulo. It's ____ a.m.

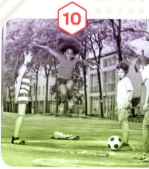

4 Make world clocks.

It's **7:30** in **Rome**.

Hands on — Planning an International Menu

1. Talk about food.

2. Look and complete.

3 Write and talk.

4 Research.

Dish: .... Country: ....

Difficult to prepare?
☐ No.
☐ A little.
☐ Very much.

How many ingredients?
☐ Up to 5.
☐ More than 5.
☐ More than 10.

Do you like it?
☐ 😋 I like it.
☐ 😝 I don't like it.
☐ 😄 I want to try it.

What it looks like:

5 Plan an international menu.

GAME 1 — Hidden Message

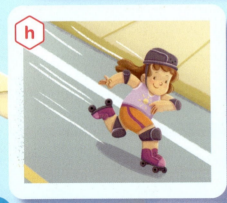

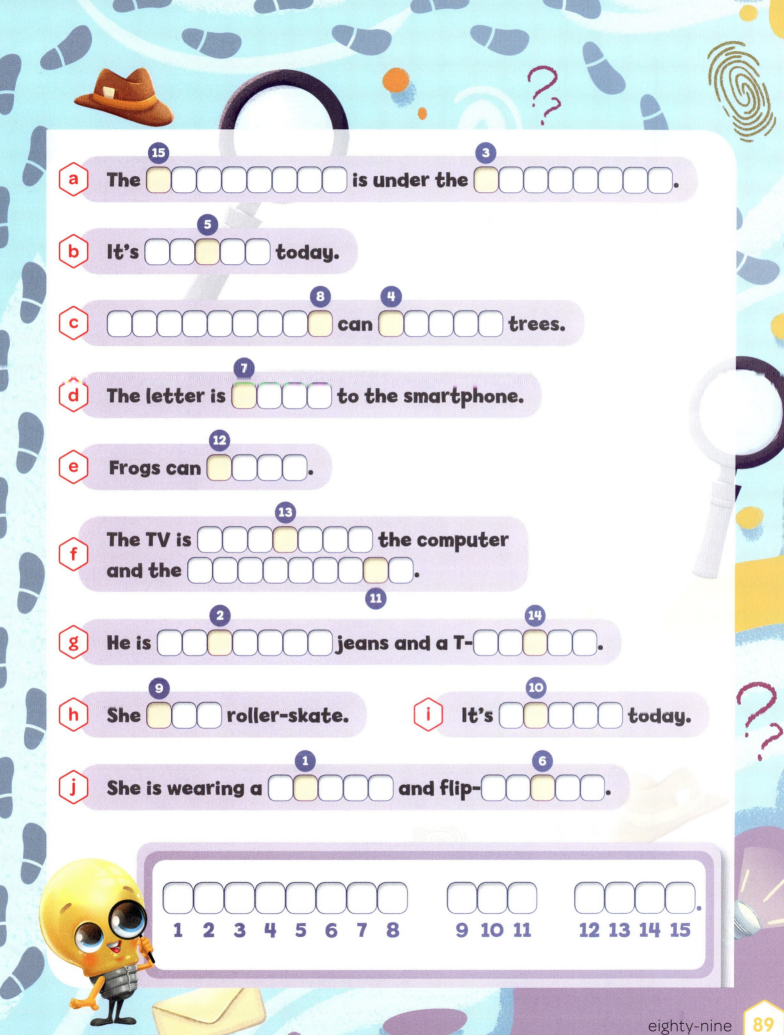

GAME 2: What Are They Doing?

ninety-one 91

Instructions

Learn more!
http://mod.lk/class3

answer: responda
be creative: seja criativo
break the code: desvende o código
calculate: calcule
check: assinale; confirme
choose: escolha
circle: circule
classify: classifique
color: pinte
complete: complete
correct: corrija
create: crie
customize: customize
describe: descreva
do: faça
draw: desenhe
find: encontre
glue: cole
guess: adivinhe
listen: ouça
look: olhe

make: faça
match: ligue, relacione
meditate: medite
mime: faça a mímica
number: numere
order: ordene
organize: organize
perform: apresente, atue
plan: planeje
play: jogue
point: aponte
practice: pratique
present: apresente
press out: destaque
read: leia
research: pesquise
role-play: encene, faça de conta
say: diga, fale
share: compartilhe
stick: cole (adesivo)
talk: converse
think: reflita, pense
underline: sublinhe
unscramble: desembaralhe
write: escreva

92 ninety-two

Language Reference

UNIT 1

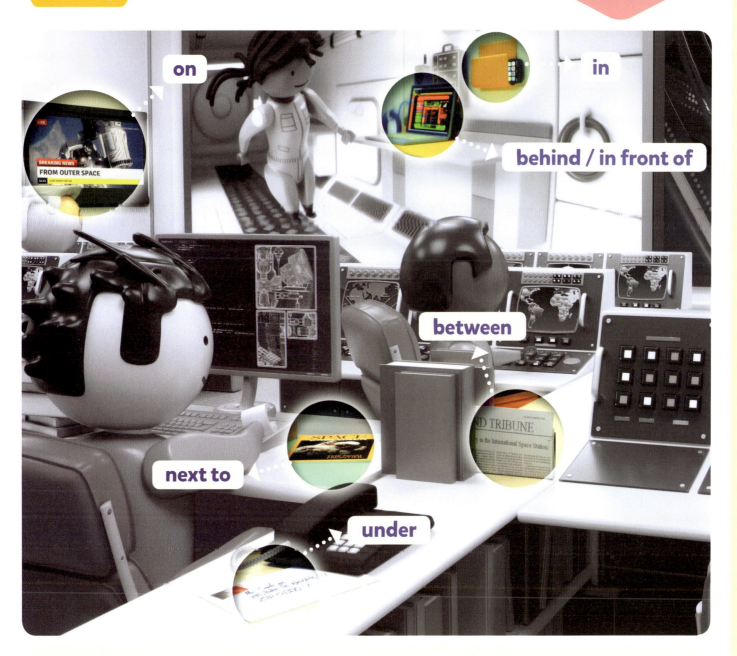

Singular

Where is the newspaper?

It's/It is between the books.

There is a newspaper between the books.

Plural

Where are the books?

They're/They are on the table.

There are books on the table.

ninety-three 93

1. Complete.

are   is   newspapers   of   smartphone   to

1 There _____ a letter on the table.

2 **A:** Where are the _____?
   B: They are next _____ the TV.

3 **A:** Where is the _____?
   B: It is in front _____ the computer.

4 There _____ telephones in the bedroom.

UNIT 2

31	thirty-one	41	forty-one	51	fifty-one	61	sixty-one
32	thirty-two	42	forty-two	52	fifty-two	62	sixty-two
33	thirty-three	43	forty-three	53	fifty-three	63	sixty-three
34	thirty-four	44	forty-four	54	fifty-four	64	sixty-four
35	thirty-five	45	forty-five	55	fifty-five	65	sixty-five
36	thirty-six	46	forty-six	56	fifty-six	66	sixty-six
37	thirty-seven	47	forty-seven	57	fifty-seven	67	sixty-seven
38	thirty-eight	48	forty-eight	58	fifty-eight	68	sixty-eight
39	thirty-nine	49	forty-nine	59	fifty-nine	69	sixty-nine
40	forty	50	fifty	60	sixty		

Wh- questions
How old is he?
How old is she?

Affirmative
He's/He is fifty-one (years old).
She's/She is thirty-nine (years old).

The temperature is 32 degrees Celsius.

What's the weather like?
It's hot and sunny.

94 ninety-four

1. Unscramble.

1 old / how / mother / is / your / ?

_____

2 today / weather / the / like / what's / ?

_____

3 old / thirty-eight / parents / my / years / are / .

_____

4 is / degrees / the / Celsius / temperature / twelve / .

_____

UNIT 3

Affirmative
I can draw.
He can roller-skate.
She can play handball.
They can dance.

Negative
I can't/cannot ride a horse.
He can't/cannot play soccer.
She can't/cannot run fast.
They can't/cannot play the guitar.

Yes-No questions
Can you ride a bike?
Can he swim?
Can she draw?
Can they climb trees?

Short answers
Yes, I can. / No, I can't.
Yes, he can. / No, he can't.
Yes, she can. / No, she can't.
Yes, they can. / No, they can't.

But
I can draw, but I can't ride a horse.
He can roller-skate, but he can't play soccer.
She can play handball, but she can't run fast.
They can dance, but they can't play the guitar.

ninety-five 95

1. Write and answer.

1. (your friend/dance)
   - ?
   - ✓

2. (you/sing)
   - ?
   - ✗

3. (Emily and Charlie/swim)
   - ?
   - ✗

4. (the teacher/draw)
   - ?
   - ✓

5. (your parents/ride a horse)
   - ?
   - ✓

UNIT 4

Adjectives before a noun

big pink sweater

old brown shoes

new colorful flip-flops

long yellow shorts

Wh- questions

What are you wearing?
What is he wearing?
What is she wearing?
What are they wearing?

Affirmative

I'm/I am wearing a long skirt.
He's/He is wearing a big sweater.
She's/She is wearing green socks.
They're/They are wearing blue jeans.

Negative

I'm not/I am not wearing new flip-flops.
He isn't/He is not wearing an old jacket.
She isn't/She is not wearing a small cap.
They aren't/They are not wearing sneakers.

Yes-No questions

Are you wearing a pink dress?
Is he wearing big shoes?
Is she wearing a new dress?
Are they wearing blue T-shirts?

Short answers

Yes, I am. / No, I'm not.
Yes, he is. / No, he isn't.
Yes, she is. / No, she isn't.
Yes, they are. / No, they aren't.

1 Complete.

1 Caroline _____ a white dress.
2 Walter and Ed _____ jeans.
3 Mike _____ (not) a cap.
4 What _____ the doctor _____ ?
5 My friends _____ (not) sweaters.
6 What _____ the teachers _____ ?
7 What _____ you _____ ?
8 I _____ a long skirt and a blue T-shirt.
9 The students _____ (not) flip-flops.

ninety-seven 97

UNIT 5

Wh- questions
What are you doing?
What is he doing?
What is she doing?
What are they doing?

Affirmative
I'm/I am playing the guitar.
He's/He is studying.
She's/She is sleeping.
They're/They are eating.

Negative
I'm not/I am not watching TV.
He isn't/He is not taking a shower.
She isn't/She is not drinking.
They aren't/They are not working.

Yes-No question
Are you studying?

Short answers
Yes, I am. / No, I'm not.

1. Correct.

1. What is the dogs doing?
2. The cat is eat.
3. Bob not is sleeping.
4. What Angelina is doing?
5. Maddie and Mae isn't cooking.
6. You are using the computer?
7. What your brother doing?
8. James aren't drinking water.

UNIT 6

What time is it?

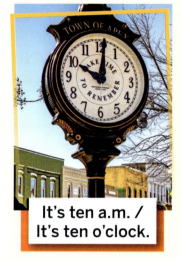
It's ten a.m. / It's ten o'clock.

It's midday.

It's ten p.m. / It's ten o'clock.

It's midnight.

It's ten o'clock p.m. and I'm going to bed.

1. Unscramble.

1 I'm / lunch / and / midday / having / it's / .

___

2 getting up / a.m. / thirty / and / seven / it's / I'm / .

___

3 forty-five / and / I'm / homework / it's / four / doing / p.m. / .

___

4 time / it / what / is / ?

___

UNIT 7

70	seventy	78	seventy-eight	86	eighty-six	94	ninety-four
71	seventy-one	79	seventy-nine	87	eighty-seven	95	ninety-five
72	seventy-two	80	eighty	88	eighty-eight	96	ninety-six
73	seventy-three	81	eighty-one	89	eighty-nine	97	ninety-seven
74	seventy-four	82	eighty-two	90	ninety	98	ninety-eight
75	seventy-five	83	eighty-three	91	ninety-one	99	ninety-nine
76	seventy-six	84	eighty-four	92	ninety-two	100	a hundred
77	seventy-seven	85	eighty-five	93	ninety-three		

a + consonant sound

a hot dog

an + vowel sound

an apple pie

Singular

How much is the cheeseburger?

It's/It is two dollars.

Plural

How much are the sandwiches?

They're/They are six dollars and fifty cents.

Singular

I'd like a soda.

I'd like an orange juice.

Plural

I'd like French fries.

1. Match.

1 I'd like a…   a ☐ the chocolate cake?
2 How much are…   b ☐ ice cream.
3 I'd like an…   c ☐ is three dollars.
4 It…   d ☐ salad.
5 How much is…   e ☐ are seven dollars.
6 They…   f ☐ the French fries?

100 a hundred

UNIT 8

Wh- questions
What is he doing?
What is she doing?
What are they doing?

Affirmative
He's/He is crossing a river.
She's/She is diving in the ocean.
They're/They are exploring a cave.

Negative
He isn't/He is not hiking in the jungle.
She isn't/She is not sailing through a swamp.
They aren't/They are not climbing a mountain.

1. Complete.

climb   cross   dive (not)   do   explore
sail (not)   swim (not)   visit

1. The children _____ the jungle.
2. Karen _____ a cave.
3. What _____ the brothers _____ ?
4. Paul _____ in the river.
5. Joey and Danny _____ in the ocean.
6. My sister _____ a boat through a swamp.
7. My friends _____ the river.
8. Tim _____ a big mountain.

Glossary

UNIT 1

avoid: evitar
behind: atrás
best: o(a) melhor
between: entre
clock: relógio
conflict: conflito
contact: contato
desk: carteira escolar
diagram: diagrama
diary: diário; agenda
evolution: evolução
from: de
in: dentro de
in front of: na frente de
key: chave
kind: tipo
letter: carta
magazine: revista
newspaper: jornal
next to: ao lado de
on: sobre, em cima de
pencil case: estojo
picture: fotografia
quiet: quieto(a)
sad: triste
schoolbag: mochila
spaceship: nave espacial
story: história
surprised: surpreso(a)
they: eles, elas
tired: cansado(a)
title: título
today: hoje
under: embaixo de
where: onde

UNIT 2

all year round: ao longo do ano
April: abril
August: agosto
calendar: calendário
celebration: dia comemorativo
cloudy: nublado(a)
cold: frio(a)
days of the week: dias da semana
December: dezembro
degree: grau (temperatura)
fall: outono
February: fevereiro
Germany: Alemanha
graph: gráfico
highest: o(a) mais alto(a)
holiday: feriado
hot: quente
January: janeiro
Japan: Japão
July: julho
June: junho
Labor Day: Dia do Trabalho
lowest: o(a) mais baixo(a)
March: março
May: maio
month: mês
November: novembro
October: outubro
parents: pais
rainy: chuvoso(a)
same: mesmo(a)
season: estação do ano
September: setembro
snowy: com neve
spring: primavera
summer: verão
sunny: ensolarado(a)
Turkey: Turquia
warm: morno(a)
weather: tempo atmosférico
weather forecast: previsão do tempo
windy: com vento
winter: inverno

UNIT 3

almost never: quase nunca
barrage: barragem, represa
bear: urso
beaver: castor
bone: osso
breath: respiração
build: construir
but: mas
can: saber; conseguir
climb: escalar, subir
cut down: derrubar (árvore)
dance: dançar
dark: escuro(a)
draw: desenhar
drums: bateria (instrumento musical)
fast: rápido(a)
fish: peixe

102 a hundred and two

forest: floresta
frog: sapo
get down: descer
guitar: violão
hare: lebre
have: ter
herbivore: herbívoro
hold: segurar
honey: mel
hours a day: horas por dia
insect: inseto
lifespan: tempo de vida
live: viver
mammal: mamífero
moose: alce(s)
move all the way around: dar uma volta completa
neck: pescoço
news article: artigo de notícia
play: jogar; tocar (instrumento musical)
raccoon: guaxinim
resilience: resiliência
ride a bike: andar de bicicleta
ride a horse: andar a cavalo
roller-skate: andar de patins
run: correr
salamander: salamandra
see: enxergar
sing: cantar
sleep: dormir
sloth: bicho-preguiça
some: algum(a), alguns/algumas
squirrel: esquilo
swim: nadar
tree: árvore
underwater: embaixo d'água
weigh: pesar
wolf: lobo

cap: boné
cause: causa
clothes: roupas
convince: convencer
darling: querido(a)
donate: doar
dress: vestido
flip-flops: chinelos de dedo
hat: chapéu
heart: coração
jacket: jaqueta
long: comprido(a), longo(a)
new: novo(a)
old: velho(a)
pass it on: passar adiante
reader: leitor(a)
ready: pronto(a)
shirt: camisa
shoes: sapatos
short: curto(a)
skirt: saia
sneakers: tênis
socks: meias
T-shirt: camiseta
wear: vestir; usar (acessório)

busy: ocupado(a)
clean: limpar
cook: cozinhar
do: fazer

drink: beber, tomar
eat: comer
help: ajudar; ajuda
improve: melhorar
indoors: ambiente interno
juice: suco
listen to music: ouvir música
meditate: meditar
movie: filme
need: precisar
now: agora
orange: laranja
outdoors: ambiente externo
properly: adequadamente
relaxing: relaxante
skateboard: andar de *skate*
song: canção
stretch: alongar-se
study: estudar
take a shower: tomar banho
talk: conversar
text message: mensagem de texto
tiger: tigre
turn: vez
understand: entender; compreender
use the computer: usar o computador
watch TV: assistir à TV
work: trabalhar

afternoon: período da tarde
bus: ônibus

a hundred and three 103

Glossary

buy: comprar
cheese: queijo
daily: diariamente
drive: dirigir; levar de carro
get up: levantar-se
go to bed: ir deitar-se
half an hour: meia hora
have breakfast: tomar café da manhã
have dinner: jantar (verbo)
have lunch: almoçar
hungry: com fome
let me know: avise-me
midday: meio-dia
midnight: meia-noite
minute: minuto
night: noite
note: bilhete
o'clock: em ponto, hora cheia
refrigerator: geladeira
second: segundo
soccer practice: treino de futebol
store: loja
time: hora
train: trem

a/an: um(a)
ad: anúncio; propaganda
apple: maçã
beverage: bebida
cent: centavo
chocolate cake: bolo de chocolate
come: vir
customer: cliente
dessert: sobremesa
French fries: batatas fritas
I'd like: Eu gostaria de
ice cream: sorvete
keychain: chaveiro
lemon: limão
like: gostar
nutritional information: informação nutricional
onion rings: anéis de cebola
open-mindedness: abertura ao novo
pancake: panqueca
pie: torta
price: preço
receipt: recibo
recipe: receita
sandwich: sanduíche
server: atendente
smoothie: vitamina
soda: refrigerante
toast: torrada
toy: brinquedo
try: experimentar
veggie burger: hambúrguer vegetariano
want: querer
yeast extract: extrato de levedura

all: todo(a)
amazing: incrível
any: qualquer
book: reservar
bridge: ponte
call: ligar
camp: acampar
cave: caverna
city: cidade
cost: custar
cross: atravessar
desert: deserto
deterioration: degradação
dive: mergulhar
enjoy: aproveitar
explore: explorar
falls: cataratas
glacier: glaciar, geleira
hike: fazer caminhada/trilha
Iceland: Islândia
jungle: selva
leaflet: panfleto
look for: procurar
most: o(a) mais
mountain: montanha
nature: natureza
ocean: oceano
paradise: paraíso
requirement: exigência
river: rio
sail: velejar
Sunday: domingo
swamp: pântano
trip: viagem; passeio
Tuesday: terça-feira
usually: geralmente
vacation: férias
visit: visitar
volcano: vulcão
waterfall: cachoeira

104 a hundred and four

Name: _____ Class: _____

Workbook UNIT 1

1 **Do the crossword puzzle.**

2 **Read and circle.**

1 **A:** Where are the **letter** / **letters**?

  B: It is / **They are** next to the computer.

2 **A:** Where is the **newspaper** / **newpapers**?

  B: It is / **They are** under the table.

a hundred and five 105

3. **Look, read and write T or F.**

1. ☐ The schoolbag is next to the desk.
2. ☐ The computer is under the desk.
3. ☐ The tablet is between the books and the clock.
4. ☐ The newspaper is on the chair.
5. ☐ The magazines are on the schoolbag.
6. ☐ The pencil case is behind the computer.

4. **Read and answer.**

1. Where is your English book?

2. Where are your colored pencils?

Name: _____ Class: _____

Workbook
UNIT 2

1 Look and write.

2 Calculate and write.

① 50 + 5 = ☐

② 31 + 12 = ☐

③ 48 - 17 = ☐

④ 33 + 25 = ☐

⑤ 78 - 18 = ☐

⑥ 66 - 40 = ☐

a hundred and seven 107

3. Look and complete.

1 It's _____.

2 It's _____.

3 It's _____.

4 It's _____.

4. Think and complete.

1 In the summer, the weather is _____.
2 In the winter, the weather is _____.
3 In the spring, the weather is _____.
4 In the fall, the weather is _____.
5 Today, the weather is _____.

108   a hundred and eight

Name: _____ Class: _____

Workbook UNIT 3

1. Look and write.

1. B _____
2. F _____
3. R _____
4. S _____

2. Look and complete.

1. _____ trees

2. _____ a bike

3. roller- _____

a hundred and nine 109

3 Read and complete.

1. A: <u>Can</u> bears climb trees?
   B: Yes, <u>they can</u>.
2. A: _____ raccoons swim?
   B: Yes, _____.
3. A: _____ your sister play handball?
   B: No, _____.

4 Read and write.

1 Ellen and David <u>can dance</u>, but they <u>can't sing</u> or <u>play soccer</u>.

2 Carrie and Max _____ and _____, but they _____.

3 Ellen, David and Max _____, but they _____.

4 I _____ and _____, but I _____ or _____.

Name: _____ Class: _____

Workbook UNIT 4

1 Look, circle and write.

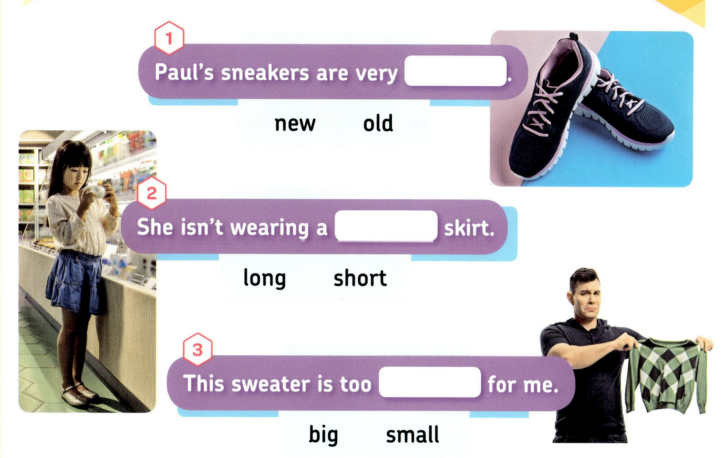

1. Paul's sneakers are very _____.
   new   old

2. She isn't wearing a _____ skirt.
   long   short

3. This sweater is too _____ for me.
   big   small

2 Read, draw and color.

1. She is wearing a long red skirt, an orange T-shirt, flip-flops and a small hat.

2. He is wearing old jeans, a green sweater, black and white sneakers and a cap.

a hundred and eleven 111

3. **Look and complete.**

Lizzie: Hi! I am calling to tell you we are ready!

Joan: Nice, Lizzie! What color are all of you (1)_____?

Lizzie: We (2)_____ wearing different colors.

Joan: (3)_____ Junior wearing flip-flops?

Lizzie: No, (4)_____. He is wearing black and white (5)_____.

Joan: Good! And (6)_____ is Travis wearing?

Lizzie: He is wearing (7)_____ shoes, a shirt and a big black (8)_____.

Joan: (9)_____ you and Andrea wearing long (10)_____?

Lizzie: Yes, (11)_____. I am wearing a (12)_____, pink and white skirt and Andrea is wearing an (13)_____ skirt.

Joan: Is (14)_____ wearing a hat?

Lizzie: Yes, she (15)_____. A (16)_____ black hat.

Joan: (17)_____ Jonas (18)_____ a white T-shirt?

Lizzie: No, (19)_____. Carl (20)_____ a white T-shirt.

Joan: That sounds fun! Send me a picture of you all, please!

Workbook

UNIT 5

Name: _____ Class: _____

1 Find and circle.

```
U S E T H E C O M P U T E R
C X P D K X V A H L Z S R I
P X Y T R R L Y C L E A N J
U L F T X I R F F Y T R W Z
B S A Z A E N T I H S R I T
C S M Y W K I K G C V P T N
X W S T V A E C G I W M S P
S Y N W H I T A S T U D Y F
L Y M O A E D C S E Z Z M T
E E Q R J W C E H H Y Z S J
E L B K T L P N O T O B D A
P Y A O H R R Y M G V W C C
X Q T A L K S I T P A S E H
X Y K H Y G I W A A W M P R
S K A T E B O A R D M T E D
R P V P E R N T C O O K E S
L I S T E N T O M U S I C R
T O E A T M B E O A R D P L
```

a hundred and thirteen 113

2 Look and correct.

1 They are studying in image 1.
_____

2 He is taking a shower in image 2.
_____

3 They are using the computer in image 11.
_____

4 She is eating pizza in image 13.
_____

3 Read and complete.

cook   eat   listen (not)
play (not)   use   watch (not)

1 William _____ lunch.

2 Val and Sylvia _____ video games.

3 Sandra and Mark _____ a sandwich.

4 Ray _____ to music.

5 Florence and Phil _____ a movie.

6 I _____ the computer.

114   a hundred and fourteen

Workbook

Name: _____ Class: _____

UNIT 6

1 Look and write.

1. It's one o'clock.

2 Break the code and answer.

thirteen = M   twenty-seven = S   thirty-eight = T   forty-four = A
eighteen = H   thirty-three = E   forty-two = I   fifty-two = W

52 18 44 38   38 42 13 33   42 27   42 38 ?

It's _____.

a hundred and fifteen 115

3 Look and complete.

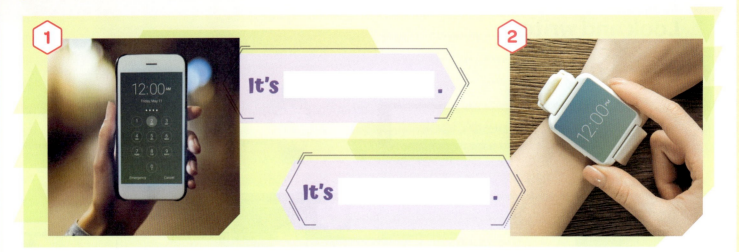

1. It's _____.
2. It's _____.

4 Match and answer.

1. ☐ What are you doing at ten a.m.?
2. ☐ What are you doing at ten thirty p.m.?
3. ☐ What are you doing at seven a.m.?
4. ☐ What are you doing at one p.m.?

Name: _____ Class: _____

Workbook
UNIT 7

1 Look and write.

2 Look and classify.

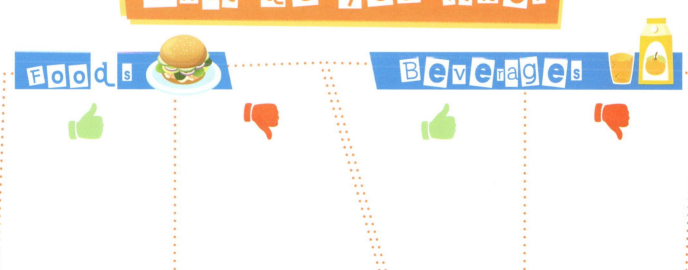

a hundred and seventeen 117

3 Complete.

1. I'd like _____ smoothie, please.
2. I'd like _____ apple juice, please.
3. I'd like _____ soda, please.
4. I'd like _____ chocolate cake, please.
5. I'd like _____ ice cream, please.

4 Read and complete.

1. A: How much is the keychain? ($5.69)
   B: It's five dollars and sixty-nine cents.

2. A: _____ the book? ($9.99)
   B: It's _____.

3. A: _____ the cheeseburgers? ($4.86)
   B: They're _____.

4. A: _____ the toys? ($7.78)
   B: They're _____.

5. A: _____ the bike? ($100.00)
   B: It's _____.

118 a hundred and eighteen

Name: _____ Class: _____

Workbook

UNIT 8

1. Check and complete.

1. My friend is _____ under the waterfall.
   - a ☐ swim
   - b ☐ crossing
   - c ☐ swimming

2. Lisa is _____ a cave.
   - a ☐ exploring
   - b ☐ diving
   - c ☐ explore

3. Allan is _____ through a swamp.
   - a ☐ dive
   - b ☐ sailing
   - c ☐ climbing

4. They are _____ in the jungle.
   - a ☐ hiking
   - b ☐ sail
   - c ☐ sailing

2. Unscramble and write.

1. is / doing / she / what / ?
   What is she doing?

2. through / is / Daphne / sailing / swamp / the / .
   _____

3. they / what / doing / are / ?
   _____

4. the / aren't / Megan and Doug / swimming / ocean / in / .
   _____

a hundred and nineteen 119

3 Look and write.

dive in the ocean / cross a river

He isn't diving in the ocean.

He's crossing a river.

swim under a waterfall / explore a cave

climb a volcano / swim under a waterfall

sail through a swamp / dive in the ocean

cross a river / hike in the jungle

explore a volcano / visit a glacier

120 a hundred and twenty

WELCOME

bakery	bathroom
bed	boat
car	chicken
couch	doctor
kitchen	library
lighthouse	plane
police officer	sad
sheep	sick

Your House

a hundred and twenty-three 123

Your Classmate's House

a hundred and twenty-five 125

UNIT 4

Press-outs

a hundred and twenty-seven 127

UNIT 1

12

Your House

Your Classmate's House

a hundred and twenty-nine

UNIT 6

REVIEW 5 & 6

UNIT 7

REVIEW 7 & 8

a hundred and thirty-three 133

Direção editorial: Sandra Possas
Edição executiva de inglês: Izaura Valverde
Edição executiva de produção e multimídia: Adriana Pedro de Almeida

Coordenação de arte e produção: Raquel Buim
Coordenação de revisão: Rafael Spigel

Edição de texto: Nathália Horvath
Elaboração de conteúdo: Carina Guiname Shiroma, Nathália Horvath
Preparação de originais: Helaine Albuquerque
Revisão: Carolina Waideman, Flora Vaz Manzione, Gisele Ribeiro Fujii, Kandy Saraiva, Márcio Martins, Ray Shoulder, Vivian Cristina de Souza

Projeto gráfico: Elaine Alves, Karina de Sá
Edição de arte: Elaine Alves
Diagramação: Casa de Ideias
Capa: Karina de Sá, Raquel Buim
Ilustração de capa: Leo Teixeira
Ilustrações: Artur Fujita, Bianca Aguiar, Fabio Eugenio, Leo Teixeira
Artes: Elaine Alves, Priscila Wu

Iconografia: Danielle de Alcântara, Paloma Klein, Sara Alencar
Coordenação de *bureau*: Rubens M. Rodrigues
Tratamento de imagens: Ademir Francisco Baptista, Joel Aparecido, Luiz Carlos Costa, Marina M. Buzzinaro, Vânia Aparecida M. de Oliveira
Pré-impressão: Alexandre Petreca, Everton L. de Oliveira, Fabio Roldan, Marcio H. Kamoto, Ricardo Rodrigues, Vitória Sousa
Áudio: Núcleo de Criação Produções em Áudio

Impressão e acabamento: HRosa Gráfica e Editora

Lote: 797801   **Cod:** 51120002163

Créditos das fotos: p. 4: ©Caíque de Abreu/Istockphoto, ©wsfurlan/Istockphoto, ©dabldy/Istockphoto, ©diegograndi/Istockphoto, ©dabldy/Istockphoto, ©Marcos Amend/Pulsar Imagens; p. 5: ©PeopleImages/Istockphoto, ©Delfim Martins/Pulsar Imagens, ©Ana Ottoni/Folhapress, ©L.C. LEITE/ESTADÃO CONTEÚDO/AE, ©diegograndi/Istockphoto; p. 6: ©sergeyryzhov/Istockphoto, ©franz12/Istockphoto, ©Serhii Lysenko/Istockphoto, ©Malkovstock/Istockphoto, ©vbacarin/Istockphoto, ©FerreiraSilva/Istockphoto, ©Istockphoto; p. 7: ©BigDuckSix/Istockphoto, ©kozmoat98/Istockphoto, ©baranozdemir/Istockphoto; p. 8: ©UNICEF, ©UNICEF, ©UNICEF, ©UNICEF, ©UNICEF, ©UNICEF, ©FG Trade/Istockphoto; p. 10: ©Larina Marina/Istockphoto, ©BrianScantlebury/Istockphoto, ©Space_cat/Istockphoto, ©Alexmia/Istockphoto, ©Portland Press Herald/Getty Images, ©Janine Lamontagne/Istockphoto, ©GideoniJunior/Istockphoto, ©Photoguns/Istockphoto, ©Delpixart/Istockphoto; p. 11: ©Monticello/Istockphoto, ©Marcos Assis/Istockphoto, ©Rawpixel/Istockphoto, ©Moyo Studio/Istockphoto, ©Nadezhda1906/Istockphoto, ©Ridofranz/Istockphoto; p. 12: ©Alamy/Fotoarena, ©monkeybusinessimages/Getty Images, ©SDI Productions/Getty Images, ©portishead1/Getty Images, ©shironosov/Getty Images; p. 13: ©helenaak/Getty Images, ©francescoridolfi/Getty Images; p. 14: ©Memedozaslan/Getty Images, ©vgajic/Getty Images, ©Zinkevych/Getty Images, ©Halfpoint/Istockphoto, ©StockPlanets/Getty Images, ©Wavebreakmedia/Getty Images, ©LSOphoto/Getty Images, ©MarsBars/Getty Images, ©Jani Bryson/Getty Images, ©Jani Bryson/Getty Images; p. 15: ©Prostock-Studio/Getty Images; p. 17: ©MIXA/Getty Images, ©VMJones/Getty Images, ©GettyImages-1127503464, ©shironosov/Istockphoto, ©mediaphotos/Getty Images.

Todos os *sites* mencionados nesta obra foram reproduzidos apenas para fins didáticos. A Richmond não tem controle sobre seu conteúdo, o qual foi cuidadosamente verificado antes de sua utilização.
Websites mentioned in this material were quoted for didactic purposes only. Richmond has no control over their content and urges care when using them.

Embora todas as medidas tenham sido tomadas para identificar e contatar os detentores de direitos autorais sobre os materiais reproduzidos nesta obra, isso nem sempre foi possível.
A editora estará pronta a retificar quaisquer erros dessa natureza assim que notificada.
Every effort has been made to trace the copyright holders, but if any omission can be rectified, the publishers will be pleased to make the necessary arrangements.

Reprodução proibida. Art. 184 do Código Penal e Lei 9.610 de 19 de fevereiro de 1998.
Todos os direitos reservados.

Richmond
Santillana Educação Ltda.
Rua Padre Adelino, 758, 3º andar – Belenzinho
São Paulo – SP – Brasil – CEP 03303-904
www.richmond.com.br
2024
Impresso no Brasil

CONTENTS

My Community 4

Ways to Improve My Community 6

Children's Rights and Responsibilities 8

Taking Care of the Environment 10

The World of Work around Me 12

The World of Work and Me 14

Social Initiative 16

Citizenship Project 18

My Community

1 Look, think and check.

2 Think and complete.

> big   coastal   historical   noisy   quiet
> rural   small   suburban   urban

I live in a/an _____ community.

3 Discuss and write.

Advantages	Disadvantages

four

FAMILY TIME!

4 Make a timeline of your community.

Step 1
Talk to your family.

Step 2
Talk to neighbors.

Step 3
Search for information.

Step 4
Organize the information.

Step 5
Make the timeline.

5 Present your timeline.

My community timeline

1985

1997

2004

2019

five 5

Ways to Improve My Community

1 Listen and number.

a crosswalk   b trash can   c street lighting

d park and playground   e bike lane   f train station

2 Think and write.

In my community...

3 Look and discuss.

1. abandoned animals

2. potholes in the street

3. no accessible sidewalks

FAMILY TIME!

4 Make a video tour around your community.

Step 1

Talk to your family.

Step 2

Plan a walk around your community.

Step 3

Walk and notice positive and negative aspects of your community.

Step 4

Make a video showing positive and negative aspects of your community.

Step 5

Watch the video.

5 Present and discuss.

Children's Rights and Responsibilities

1 Read and match.

1 Children have the right to identity.
2 Children have the right to be with their parents.
3 Children have the right to share opinions.
4 Children have the right to have information.
5 Children have the right to food, clothing and a safe place to live.
6 Children have the right to education.
7 Children have the right to rest, relax and play.

a FOOD, CLOTHING, A SAFE HOME

b KEEPING FAMILIES TOGETHER

c ACCESS TO EDUCATION

d IDENTITY

e SHARING THOUGHTS FREELY

f REST, PLAY, CULTURE, ARTS

g ACCESS TO INFORMATION

Adapted from <https://www.unicef.org/media/60981/file/convention-rights-child-text-child-friendly-version.pdf>. Accessed on February 25, 2021.

2 Read, think and draw.

Right

Children have the right to good medical service

Responsibility

... and the responsibility to take care of themselves.

Adapted from <https://www.unicef.org/uganda/media/5591/file/UGDA%20CRC%20child%20friendly%20booklet%20final.pdf>. Accessed on February 25, 2021.

8 eight

3 **Think and discuss.**

FAMILY TIME!

4 **Let's play a game.**

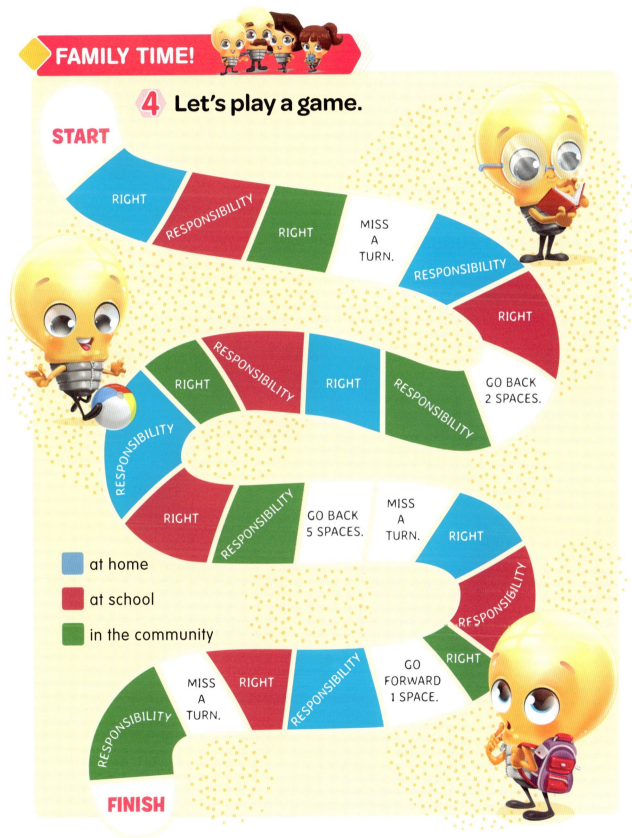

Taking Care of the Environment

1 Look and talk.

2 Look and guess.

3 Think and discuss.

transportation   trash   trees   water   wild animals

FAMILY TIME!

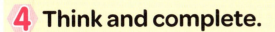

4 Think and complete.

	Very Good	Good	OK	Needs Improvement
Reduction of plastic				
Use of transportation				
Production of trash				
Use of water				
Care for trees and wild animals				

Step 1

Think about your consumption of plastic.

Step 2

Analyze your use of transportation.

Step 3

Reflect on your trash production.

Step 4

Think about your use of water.

Step 5

Analyze how you take care of trees and wild animals.

Step 6

Talk to your family about improvements.

5 Present your chart.

eleven 11

The World of Work around Me

1 Look and talk.

2 Think and draw.

In my family

3 Share and talk.

12 twelve

FAMILY TIME!

4 Go on a Work Day.

Step 1
Talk to your family and plan a Work Day.

Step 2
Prepare for your Work Day.

Step 3
Pay attention to the tasks and the routine.

Step 4
Ask questions.

Step 5
Try it out.

Step 6
Reflect on the experience.

5 Talk about your experience.

thirteen 13

The World of Work and Me

1 **Think and circle.**

Robotics club

Drama and Music club

Volunteer club

Running club

Events club

Book club

2 **Look, check and talk.**

1. I like to be active.
2. I like to be alone.
3. I like to solve problems.
4. I like to help people.

3 **Share and discuss.**

14 fourteen

FAMILY TIME!

4 Research and make a fact file.

Step 1 Talk to your family about your interests and the tasks you like.

Step 2 Talk to your family about your characteristics.

Step 3 Talk to your family about the occupations that interest you.

Step 4 Select an occupation.

Step 5 Research into the occupation.

Step 6 Write a fact file about the occupation.

5 Share your fact file.

NUTRITIONIST

What they do:	Plan food and nutrition programs, supervise the preparation and serving of meals, help prevent and treat health problems.
What they study:	Nutrition
How long they study:	4 years
Where they study:	University
Where they work:	Hospitals, clinics and private offices
Characteristics:	Be attentive, like people, have good organization.

fifteen 15

Social Initiative

1 Ask and answer.

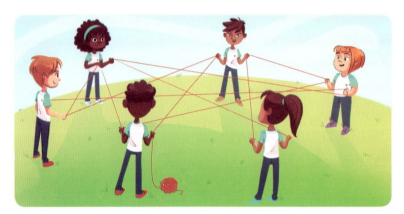

2 Think and write.

My classmate's name	What I know now about them
....	....
....	....
....	....
....	....

3 Write and draw.

My feelings	My thoughts

4 Think and talk.

16 sixteen

FAMILY TIME!

5 Role-play.

Step 1 Talk to your family.

Step 2

Role-play an elevator situation.

Step 3

Role-play a social situation.

Step 4

Role-play a playground situation.

Step 5

Role-play a classroom situation.

Step 6 Reflect on your experience.

6 Share your experience.

seventeen 17

Citizenship Project

1 **Think and check.**

FAMILY TIME!

2 **Talk and complete.**

Step 1 Talk to your family about citizenship.

Step 2 Complete the charts.

WHAT MY FAMILY DOES	WHAT MY FAMILY WANTS TO DO

3 Share and make a list.

4 Choose and plan your project.

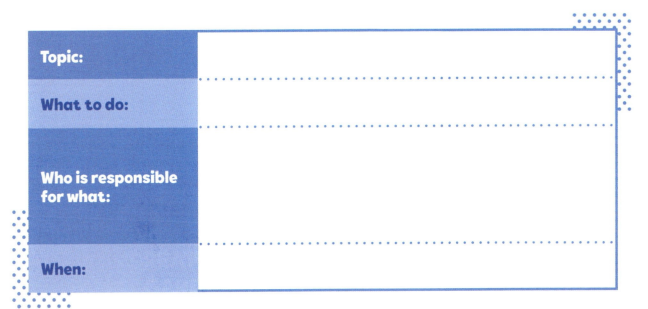

Topic:

What to do:

Who is responsible for what:

When:

5 Write a draft.

6 Put your project into practice.

nineteen 19

Learn how to identify **fake news** in a fun and simple way and raise awareness of this topic with your family and friends!

Create an account on **Richmond Educational Portal** to have access to **Digital Academy for Kids**.

www.richmond.com.br

THE BIG IDEA
English for Kids

Life Project é um dos componentes de **The Big Idea: English for Kids**, a nova coleção de língua inglesa para os anos iniciais do Ensino Fundamental. Esse componente tem como objetivo começar a desenvolver o protagonismo dos alunos e a elaboração do seu projeto de vida por meio de atividades de autoconhecimento e do trabalho com competências socioemocionais. Ele é organizado por temas que partem do âmbito individual até chegar a assuntos relacionados à atuação em sociedade e ao protagonismo dos alunos da seguinte forma:

- 1º e 2º anos trabalham assuntos relacionados à identidade dos alunos, com vistas a ampliar seu autoconhecimento;
- 3º e 4º anos abordam temáticas da vida social e da cidadania;
- 5º ano busca retomar o trabalho realizado nos volumes anteriores para os alunos exercitarem o próprio protagonismo na resolução de problemas reais.

Além disso, cada unidade de **Life Project** apresenta uma proposta de atividade para o aluno fazer em casa, junto com a família, com o intuito de aproximar visões e expectativas da família e da escola. As orientações para a realização dessas atividades encontram-se no Portal Educacional Richmond <www.richmond.com.br>.